OLD TESTAMENT GUIDES

General Editor
R.N. Whybray

1 & 2 SAMUEL

D1073435

Related titles published by JSOT Press include:

THE FATE OF KING SAUL:
AN INTERPRETATION OF A BIBLICAL STORY
David M. Gunn

THE STORY OF KING DAVID:
GENRE AND INTERPRETATION
David M. Gunn

THE DEUTERONOMISTIC HISTORY
Martin Noth

THE DOUBLE REDACTION OF
THE DEUTERONOMISTIC HISTORY
Richard D. Nelson

1 & 2
SAMUEL

R.P. Gordon

JSOT Press

For Ruth

Copyright © 1984 JSOT Press

Published by
JSOT Press
Department of Biblical Studies
The University of Sheffield
Sheffield S10 2TN
England

Printed in Great Britain
by Dotesios (Printers) Ltd.,
Bradford-on-Avon, Wiltshire.

British Library Cataloguing in Publication Data

Gordon, R.P.
    1 and 2 Samuel.—(Old Testament Guides,
    ISSN 0264-6498; v. 2)
    1. Bible. O.T. Samuel—Commentaries
    I. Title   II. Series
    222'.407   BS1325.3

    ISBN 0-905774-64-7

CONTENTS

PREFACE

THE MATERIAL in this little volume was originally intended to serve as an introduction to an, as yet, unpublished commentary on 1 and 2 Samuel. When both introduction and commentary began to look somewhat overgrown, it seemed advisable to try to publish the introduction on its own. I am, therefore, most grateful to Professor R.N. Whybray, as also to my good friends at Sheffield, for welcoming this errant child into their new series. I also gratefully acknowledge Professor Whybray's expert editorial labours on my behalf—and on the behalf of the student constituency for whom the series is intended. Thanks are also due to V. Philips Long, currently working with me on Samuel, for his helpful comments, and for many a profitable discussion of issues relating to the books of Samuel.

My wife Ruth, to whom I already owe so much, typed the manuscript most efficiently; it is to her that the finished article is affectionately dedicated.

Foxton, Cambridge, December 1982   R.P.G.

Abbreviations

AOTS	*Archaeology and Old Testament Study* (ed. D.W. Thomas, Oxford: Clarendon Press, 1967)
ASTI	*Annual of the Swedish Theological Institute*
ATANT	Abhandlungen zur Theologie des Alten und Neuen Testaments
BASOR	*Bulletin of the American Schools of Oriental Research*
BKAT	Biblischer Kommentar, Altes Testament
Botterweck— Ringgren	G.J. Botterweck and H. Ringgren (ed.), *Theological Dictionary of the Old Testament* (Grand Rapids: Eerdmans. Eng. rev. edn, 1977-)
BWANT	Beiträge zur Wissenschaft vom Alten und Neuen Testament
BZ	Biblische Zeitschrift
BZAW	Beihefte zur *Zeitschrift für die alttestamentliche Wissenschaft*
Carlson	R.A. Carlson, *David, the Chosen King* (1964)
CBQ	*Catholic Biblical Quarterly*
Childs	B.S. Childs, *Introduction to the Old Testament as Scripture* (Philadelphia: Fortress / London: SCM Press, 1979)
CMHE	*Canaanite Myth and Hebrew Epic* (F.M. Cross, 1973)
Crüsemann	F. Crüsemann, *Der Widerstand gegen das Königtum* (1978)
diss.	dissertation
Dynastie	*Die ewige Dynastie* (T. Veijola, 1975)
ET	English translation
EvTh	*Evangelische Theologie*
FRLANT	Forschungen zur Religion und Literatur des Alten und Neuen Testaments
Fs	Festschrift
Gray	J. Gray, *I and II Kings* (OTL; London: SCM Press, 2nd edn, 1970)
Hayes— Miller	J.H. Hayes and J.M. Miller (ed.), *Israelite and Judaean History* (OTL; Philadelphia: Westminster / London: SCM Press, 1977)
HUCA	*Hebrew Union College Annual*
IOSCS	International Organization for Septuagint and Cognate Studies
Ishida	T. Ishida, *The Royal Dynasties in Ancient Israel* (1977)
JAOS	*Journal of the American Oriental Society*
JBL	*Journal of Biblical Literature*
JNSL	*Journal of Northwest Semitic Languages*
JSOT	*Journal for the Study of the Old Testament*
KHAT	Kurzgefasstes exegetisches Handbuch zum Alten Testament
McCarter	P.K. McCarter, Jr, *I Samuel* (Anchor Bible 8, 1980)

Select List of Commentaries

Ackroyd, P.R.   *The First Book of Samuel; The Second Book of Samuel* (Cambridge Bible Commentary), 2 vols, Cambridge: CUP, 1971, 1977

Hertzberg, H.W.   *I and II Samuel* (OTL), London: SCM Press, 1964

Mauchline, J.   *1 and 2 Samuel* (New Century Bible), London: Oliphants, 1971

McCarter, P.K., Jr   *I Samuel* (Anchor Bible, 8), New York: Doubleday, 1980

McKane, W.   *I and II Samuel* (Torch Bible Commentaries), London: SCM Press, 1963

Stoebe, H.J.   *Das erste Buch Samuelis* (Kommentar zum Alten Testament, VIII/1), Gütersloh: Gerd Mohn, 1973

Stolz, F.   *Das erste und zweite Buch Samuel* (Zürcher Bibelkommentare, AT, 9), Zurich: Theologischer Verlag, 1981

Note on the Bibliographies

Details of works referred to are normally given in the Further Reading section at the end of the appropriate chapter, references in the text itself being confined to the author's surname, followed by the date of publication where more than one study by the same author is cited.

INTRODUCTION

THERE IS much more to the books of Samuel than the story of how Lilliput took on Brobdingnag—and won!—when David of Bethlehem felled Goliath of Gath with a well-aimed stone from his shepherd's sling (1 Sam. 17). For, in fact, 1 and 2 Samuel chronicle a structural change within Israelite society which had the profoundest political and religious consequences. At the beginning the situation differs little from what is described in the book of Judges: Israel is a loose federation of tribes owing allegiance to their common God Yahweh, and attention focuses on Shiloh as the sanctuary currently housing the ark of God. By journey's end, however, we are confronted by a centralized kingdom at the heart of what was, by ancient standards, nothing short of an empire.

Already in the time of the Judges the apostles of monarchical rule were in good voice, and we read of Gideon, hero of the famous Midianite encounter, putting a Cromwellian veto on a suggestion that he should assume royal powers (Jdg. 8:22f.). There was even a short-lived royalist experiment at Shechem, but it can scarcely have redounded to the glory of the monarchical idea (Jdg. 9). More influential, however, than any hankering after the prestige of monarchy as it existed in adjacent states was the Israelites' desire for immunity from attack by hostile neighbours like the Midianites and the Philistines. A king would be able to weld the disparate tribal elements into an effective fighting force sufficient to deter and, when necessary, defeat those who sought to pillage and to subjugate them. And assuredly as the Philistine pressure and encroachments continued, so too did the campaign for an Israelite monarchy. That was how it came about that Samuel, the last of the Judges, found himself a contemporary of Israel's first king. But because the monarchy was a controversial issue, not only at the beginning but throughout its existence, the pros and cons of the new institution are argued through six chapters in 1 Samuel (chs 7-12). There too the limits of kingly power are set forth, and, in particular, the position of the king vis-à-vis God's spokesmen the prophets and the commands that they issued in his name.

The institution of monarchy in the ancient near east, though as vulnerable to the coup as have been its modern equivalents in that part of the world, was no stranger to the principle of hereditary succession, and nowhere was this more true than in the kingdom of Judah which, apart from one unscheduled interruption (2 Kgs 11:1-16), was ruled throughout its history by the house of David. That Saul, the first occupant of the throne of Israel, had failed to establish a dynasty was therefore cause for reflection. It was not even as if Jonathan, the son who might have been expected to rule in succession to Saul, was an unfit candidate; few characters in Old Testament historical narrative are accorded such unalloyed sympathy as is Jonathan in 1 Samuel. With this in mind we can better understand why it is that, in two of the three chapters that may properly be called the account of the reign of Saul, his failure is linked with the fundamental sin of disobedience in relation to divine commands mediated through the prophet Samuel (1 Sam. 13; 15). There is, then, in Old Testament terms, an analogy between the first man and the first king of Israel, for whom also 'disobedience and the fruit / Of that forbidden tree' brought 'loss of Eden' (Milton, *Paradise Lost*, I). Saul, in this respect, may be taken as paradigmatic of kingship in Judah and Israel from the division of the kingdom to the exile. For, though Israel had disavowed the theocratic concept, the prophets would never concede that its rulers were autonomous; and, when it came to explaining the downfall of the two kingdoms, this was done, not in terms of political and military ineptitude, but of the bedrock issues of morality and religion.

So Jonathan the heir apparent had been only heir presumptive. The man who actually succeeded Saul on the throne was David son of Jesse, under whom Israel embarked upon its *grand siècle*. Militarily the times were propitious for a man with David's energy and expansionist ambitions, since the early Iron Age (from c. 1200 BC) found the great powers of the near east in temporary eclipse; for two—the Hittites and the Mitannians—the eclipse was indeed permanent. While, therefore, David had to establish his empire by conquest of most of Syro-Palestine, he did not have to worry about inviting the attentions of a Mesopotamian giant like Assyria, as did some of his successors when tempted to relatively minor ventures. Nevertheless, among undeniable successes was the subjugation of the 'old enemy', the Philistines, who at times had posed a threat to the very existence of Israel.

The creation of an Israelite kingdom and empire brought other developments in its wake—the rise of a state bureaucracy, for example, and a system of taxation which, by the end of the tenth century, had helped to drive the northern and southern halves of the kingdom irreconcilably apart. These features are observable already in David's reign, even though they did not assume the Solomonic proportions that were to bring them into such serious disrepute. There were rebellions too, and a temporary ousting from Jerusalem of the king-emperor; it is, indeed, a remarkable fact that the bulk of the Davidic tradition in 2 Samuel relates, not to David's conquests and imperial administration, but to dark episodes in the history of the royal family, and, in particular, to the rebellion against David headed by his own son Absalom. In the so-called 'Succession Narrative' which treats of these themes, historical and literary interests combine to produce a surprisingly candid portrait of David, in which the man and the parent threaten to destroy the king. This is the more noteworthy when we consider the probability that the Succession Narrative was composed within court circles. Later generations educated in the ideology of Davidic Messianism could not but be aware that the Davidic colossus had clayey feet. Since, moreover, it was seldom otherwise with the Davidic line, it is a point of the greatest significance that the frank portraiture of the Succession Narrative is prefaced by the 'dynastic oracle' of 2 Samuel 7, with its unconditional assurance of a perpetual Davidic dynasty; for, not the weak and erring descendants of David, but the word of God first declared by his prophet Nathan was to be the ground of Israel's hope during the monarchy.

The capture of Jerusalem, the last-remaining Canaanite enclave in Israelite territory, and its designation as the capital of David's kingdom, was a master-stroke, and one of the concerns of the Samuel narrative is to show how religious supremacy passed from the Elide shrine at Shiloh to Jerusalem. In that connection much is made of the ark of God and of its procession, midst great jubilation, to a specially-prepared tent in Jerusalem (2 Sam. 6:1-22). Tantalizingly, the conclusion of 2 Samuel leaves us at the threshing-floor of Araunah, where David's sacrifice appeased the census plague, without actually saying—as does the Chronicler (1 Chr. 22:1)—that this is the site of the future temple.

Composition of 1 and 2 Samuel

With the compilation of the books of Samuel the prophet Samuel can
have had nothing to do, if only because his death is recorded already
at 1 Samuel 25:1 in the context of Saul's reign. The naming of Old
Testament books, whether in Jewish or Christian tradition, is a
matter of some indifference: in the Septuagint translation the Books
of Samuel were taken together with 1 and 2 Kings to make four
'Books of Kingdoms (or 'Reigns')'. That 1 and 2 Samuel comprise a
number of sources which have been linked together to form a
continuous narrative climaxing in the reign of David is a perfectly
reasonable conjecture. In the present century the identification of
three originally independent narratives—the Ark Narrative, the
History of David's Rise, and the Succession Narrative—has gained
wide acceptance and, whatever we may think of the supporting
arguments, certainly provides for a convenient break-down of the
greater part of the material in these books. In addition, traditions
concerning Shiloh, the beginnings of the monarchy, and the reigns of
Saul and David have been interspersed to help make up the colourful
literary, theological, and historical montage that is 1 and 2 Samuel.
Because these fifty-five chapters have much more than the mere
recital of historical facts as their aim, and in concession to the overtly
theological-interpretative interests of the underlying sources and
traditions, discussion of historical questions is subsumed under
literary-narrative rubrics in the survey that follows.

A Note on the Text

The text of the Old Testament has survived the hazards of transmission relatively unimpaired, as was well illustrated when the complete
scroll of Isaiah found at Qumran was published. But unfortunately
the books of Samuel must be judged the poor relation in this regard,
in view of the number of errors, especially haplographic errors (in
this case usually the accidental omission of material between adjacent
occurrences of the same word(s), or of words similar in appearance)
which they harbour. This, it must be said, still affects only a tiny
proportion of the overall text and acts more as a challenge than as an
irritant to the text-critic and commentator. For a long time the value
of the Greek Septuagint translation of Samuel—used with circum-
spection and with proper regard for recensional questions that
cannot begin to be discussed here—as an aid for the recovery of

original readings has been recognized and gratefully accepted by most scholars. It was therefore a most welcome turn of fortune when a number of Hebrew fragments of Samuel, two millennia old, were found in Cave 4 at Qumran in the early 1950s. These fragments, still awaiting official publication (though highly photogenic in the meantime!), often align with readings that had already been reconstructed on the basis of the Septuagint and are invaluable for the study of the early history of the text of Samuel.

Further Reading

For general discussion of the fragments of Samuel from Qumran and their significance see:

E. Tov, 'The Textual Affiliations of 4QSam^{a}', *JSOT* 14 (1979), 37-53.

F.M. Cross, Jr, *The Ancient Library of Qumran and Modern Biblical Studies* (rev. edn), Grand Rapids: Baker Book House, 1980.

The most useful assemblage (to date) of readings from the fragments will be found in:

E.C. Ulrich, Jr, *The Qumran Text of Samuel and Josephus* (Harvard Semitic Monographs, 19), Missoula: Scholars Press, 1978.

Various technical aspects are discussed by a number of scholars in:

E. Tov (ed.), *The Hebrew and Greek Texts of Samuel. 1980 Proceedings IOSCS—Vienna*, Jerusalem: Academon, 1980.

There is much helpful information and discussion in McCarter's commentary; see pp. 5-11 ('Text and Versions'), as well as appropriate points throughout the commentary.

1

THE DEUTERONOMISTIC
HISTORY

The Former Prophets

1 AND 2 SAMUEL are placed in the prophetic division of the tripartite Hebrew canon (cf. Lk. 24:44), being reckoned together with Joshua, Judges, and Kings as 'The Former Prophets'. This expression occurs twice in the Old Testament (Zech. 1:4; 7:7) in reference to the classical prophets of the pre-exilic era, but its use as a canonical term is distinctly post-biblical. Since the classification of Joshua–2 Kings in this way can scarcely be intended as a reflection of the importance of the prophets in these books—Kings, as a matter of fact, has remarkably little to say about the classical prophets—it may usefully be interpreted as a statement about the determinative role of the custodial prophetic word in Israel's history. Upon Israel's response to the message of authentic prophecy depends her right to exist before God; the consistent teaching of these books is that when the prophetic word is not heard and obeyed Israel will come under the disciplinary hand of God. That, in spite of the prophets, was how things worked out, and the spirits of the prophets attend the obsequies for both the northern and southern kingdoms as 'The Former Prophets' reach their conclusion (2 Kgs 17:13-23; 24:1-4).

From Conquest to Captivity

More recent still than the concept of the 'Former Prophets' is that of the 'Deuteronomistic History' as propounded by Martin Noth in his highly influential *Überlieferungsgeschichtliche Studien I*, published in 1943. Whereas the custom had been to treat Joshua–2 Kings as so many books individually redacted to exemplify the theological principles set forth in Deuteronomy, Noth developed his thesis of a continuous history of Israel from the settlement in Canaan to the demise of Judah in the early sixth century BC, the work of a single Deuteronomistic compiler who, apart from using a variety of sources and archival records, freely inserted his own comments and amplifications, and was responsible for the overall structure of the history. This history did not, in fact, begin at Joshua 1:1, for Noth reckoned that the book of Deuteronomy in its present form includes a substantial prologue (Dt. 1-3[4]) and a supplement (parts of Dt. 31-34) whose primary function is in relation to the ensuing history rather than to the Deuteronomic laws and exhortations which they encase. Because the Deuteronomistic History ends with a notice concerning the release from prison of Jehoiachin, sometime king of Judah (2 Kgs 25:27-30), Noth held that the work was compiled, in Judah, soon after 562 BC and before the decree of Cyrus in 538 BC. As to the purpose of this major historiographical enterprise, Noth expressed himself in what have come to be regarded as unduly negative terms: the Deuteronomist viewed the downfall of Judah as final and irreversible, and sought to justify this act of divine retribution to the generation of the exile by reminding them of the causes, as also of the repeated warnings of danger that had been sounded by the prophets. Of a proffered hope of restoration, however, Noth saw not a glimmer—not even in the Jehoiachin codicil.

Noth's Deuteronomistic hypothesis has more or less become an 'assured result' of Old Testament criticism, though some of his successors in the field have gone in for more complex models. While his central thesis of a large-scale history written to Deuteronomistic specifications has had an impressive number of subscribers, the manner of the composition of the History, its date, provenance, and purpose have each been the subject of alternative explanations. The possibility of two, or even three, editions of the History—so accounting for certain tensions within the Deuteronomistic theology—has been explored by a number of writers, particularly along the lines of pre-exilic composition and exilic redaction (J. Gray, F.M. Cross, R.D. Nelson, R.E. Friedman). Can it be shown, for example, that the expression 'to this day', which is especially common in contemporizing references in 1 and 2 Kings, occurs not only in archival material but also in editorial (Deuteronomistic, presumably) commentary? The question, which is an old one as far as Kings is concerned, has naturally been revived in discussions of the larger work which *ex hypothesi* includes 1 and 2 Kings. Cross singles out the occurrences of 'to this day' in 2 Kings 8:22 and 16:6 as being both pre-exilic and Deuteronomistic, though he does not pursue the point with much conviction. A more important consideration for Cross is the evident vitality of the 'Davidic hope' in the Deuteronomistic History, and the need to identify the circumstances in which it is most likely to have blossomed forth. Since the Babylonian exile fails to provide the right conditions, but more especially in view of the Deuteronomistic portrayal of Josiah as a David *redivivus*, fulfilling the Davidic ideal and reactivating the dynastic promise, Cross anchors the first edition of the History in the reign of Josiah (c. 640-609 BC). This first edition, he argues, had a definite propagandist purpose related to the aims of the Josianic reformation:

> In particular, the document speaks to the North, calling Israel to
> return to Judah and to Yahweh's sole legitimate shrine in Jerusalem,
> asserting the claims of the ancient Davidic monarchy upon all Israel
> (p. 284).

That Josiah was the latter-day hero of the History certainly seems obvious from the manner in which his reforms are reported there, and from the nonpareil eulogy of 2 Kings 23:25 ('there was no king like him')—worded in such a way as to recall the encomium on Moses himself (cf. Dt. 34:10ff.). Hardly less significant is the strategic mention of Josiah's name in 1 Kings 13:2, three centuries ahead of time, immediately after the account of the disruption of the united kingdom of Israel. The first clause is even faintly messianic in tone:

> Behold, a son shall be born to the house of David, Josiah by name;
> and he shall sacrifice upon you the priests of the high places who
> burn incense upon you, and men's bones shall be burned upon you.

All things considered, Cross has made out an attractive case for dating the original Deuteronomistic History to Josiah's reign. If his excision of material which appears to 'conditionalize' the Davidic hope prior to Josiah's reign strikes us as cavalier, it is also, as Nelson's retouches show, largely unnecessary.

A different approach to the redaction issue is represented by W. Dietrich and T. Veijola, both of whom operate with a three-tiered system in which an exilic Deuteronomistic History is revised, first to promote certain prophetic interests ('prophetic redaction'), and then later to highlight the requirement of compliance with the Mosaic law ('nomistic redaction'). To take an example: Veijola (1977) is by no means alone in treating 1 Samuel 7 as substantially a Deuteronomistic composition, but he introduces the refinement of assigning verses 2-4 to the 'nomistic' redaction for the reason that God's deliverance of Israel is made contingent upon their repudiation of foreign gods. What these scholars appear to be doing, however, is classifying texts according to subject-matter rather than providing real evidence of redactional activity in accordance with the principles outlined. Veijola's 1975 study, it should be noted, has few sympathizers in its claim to find evidence of large-scale Deuteronomistic redaction in the books of Samuel (see below).

Time has shown that Noth's statement of the purpose of the Deuteronomistic History is the least convincing aspect of his theory. The idea that a literary undertaking of these dimensions should have no other purpose than the explanation of past events to a generation bereft of a future has simply failed to impress most of Noth's scholarly compeers. Moreover, his objection to interpreting 2 Kings 25:27-30 as hinting at the possibility of national restoration has been met with equally confident assertions on the other side, these based, in a few cases, upon a close examination of the verses in question (so, e.g., Zenger). Noth has also been faulted for failing to do justice to the Davidic hope as it is expressed in the History, not only in the 'dynastic oracle' of 2 Samuel 7, but at various points leading up to, and away from, that ideological summit. If the dynastic promise was unconditional and was not rescinded (cf. Nelson), then the exile cannot be the full stop that Noth made it out to be. A similar message may be derived from the scheme of apostasy—judgment—repentance—deliverance which is outlined in Judges 2:10-23 and whose interpretative force may well extend beyond that book—perhaps even as a key for the unlocking of 2 Kings 25:27-30. Nor should we overlook the various passages outside Judges where the efficacy of repentance, even when the sinner is a north Israelite king (1 Kgs 21:29), is maintained. That so much in the Deuteronomistic History is of a kerygmatic nature also seems to suggest a degree of open-endedness with regard to the future: from the warnings and pleadings of the prophets Israel, even in exile, may know that God's banished are not expelled from him. Accordingly, H.W. Wolff has characterized the History as an extended sermon which, in reviewing Israel's past, seeks to apply the lessons of that past and challenge the generation of the exile, which first came across the History in more or less its final form, to repent and experience Yahweh's favour once again.

Deuteronomistic Editing in Samuel

Deuteronomistic editing in the books of Samuel is, by common agreement, slight in comparison with the other books that make up the
Deuteronomistic History, the probable reason for this being that the
Deuteronomistic compiler was working with large literary blocks,
such as the 'Succession Narrative', which he saw fit to join together
with minimal editorial comment inserted or appended. Veijola's claim
of a more pervasive Deuteronomistic presence in Samuel has already
been noted, and may not unfairly be regarded as reflective of the
imperialist tendencies of the phenomenon of Deuteronomism in current
Old Testament study—a trend which has met with something less
than universal acclaim, it must also be said. Apart from phraseological
criteria (see Weinfeld's 'Appendix A'), the Deuteronomistic hand is
recognized in the prominence given to such theological tenets as the
authority of Deuteronomic law, the determinative role of prophecy in
history, the Davidic covenant, and the primacy of the Jerusalem
temple. Little among these concerns, it will be observed, is peculiar to
the Deuteronomistic History, and it is important to bear this in mind
when labelling a phrase, verse, or section 'Deuteronomistic'.

We have already remarked upon the significance of repentance in
the Deuteronomistic scheme of things, and particularly on its
potential as a source of hope for the future. In two passages in
1 Samuel, both of them commonly regarded as evincing Deuteronomistic influence, this restorative effect of repentance is illustrated.
The first is the story of Israel's victory over the Philistines at
Ebenezer, which begins with Samuel challenging his fellow-Israelites
to a proper commitment to Yahweh, and assuring them of relief from
Philistine oppression 'if you are *returning* to the LORD with all your
heart' (1 Sam. 7:3). Here the Hebrew verb *šûb* virtually means 'to
come in repentance', and the remainder of the chapter tells how,
having done exactly that, the Israelites witnessed a famous victory.
The key verb is not used in 1 Samuel 12, but the same message comes
through: Samuel denounces the people for their great wickedness in
demanding a king (vv. 6-18), they confess their wrong (v. 19), and on
that basis are offered the hope of a continuing relationship with
Yahweh (vv. 20-24). Nevertheless, they are warned in a parting shot
that persistence in the old ways will bring only ruin (v. 25).

Noth regarded 1 Samuel 7:2–8:22 and 12:1-25 as thoroughly
Deuteronomistic compositions—a sort of black edging to the section

on the monarchy, leaving no doubt as to the Deuteronomistic editor's disenchantment with that institution. The prevalent tendency nowadays, however, is to distinguish between pre-Deuteronomistic and Deuteronomistic material in these chapters. Thus in ch. 7 Birch finds evidence of Deuteronomistic redaction in verses 3f. and 13f. only, while P. Weimar (*Biblica* 57 [1976], 66) traces the bulk of verses 7-11 to a pre-Deuteronomistic 'Yahweh War' account. In similar vein, McCarter envisages a prophetic substratum which has been given a Deuteronomistic overlay as a means of integrating the Samuel tradition into the Deuteronomistic theology of history. It is much the same with ch. 8. Contrasting significantly with Noth's pan-Deuteronomism are A. Weiser's estimation of the chapter as a historically-based tradition from Ramah, Samuel's native city, and F. Crüsemann's dating of verses 11-18 to the period of the early monarchy.

It is generally agreed that 1 Samuel 12 is the chapter where the Deuteronomistic hand is most in evidence. It contains a speech by Samuel which Noth included among the great orations inserted by the Deuteronomist to mark turning-points in Israel's history, in this case the transition from the theocracy of the period of the Judges to monarchy. In this speech Samuel reviews the saving acts of God on Israel's behalf under the old order, and lays down the conditions which must be fulfilled if this help is to be enjoyed in the future. (Because of this emphasis Veijola [1977] attributes the whole chapter to his 'nomistic redactor'.) Again, however, something less than the entire chapter is attributed to Deuteronomistic creativity by such representative scholars as Birch, Stoebe, and McCarter. But, whatever the minutiae of the various analyses, it remains perfectly clear that, from the Deuteronomistic point of view, Israel's monarchy was conceived in sin; attempts to relieve the Deuteronomistic outlook of its anti-monarchical animus (e.g. Birch) are ill-judged.

No discussion of Deuteronomistic influence in Samuel should omit reference to 2 Samuel 7. Deuteronomistic representation in the chapter is frequently asserted—but is it limited to the (apparent) instance of 'name theology' in verse 13a, or is the chapter 'swarming' (Cross) with Deuteronomisms? Perhaps the wisest course is to follow McCarthy who, leaving aside the details of source analysis, emphasizes that the chapter is integral to the structure of the Deuteronomistic History. (The importance of 2 Samuel 7 is acknowledged in the present volume by the allocation of a separate chapter to it.) In short, McCarthy aims to repair an omission by Noth, claiming for the

Nathan dynastic oracle a place among the hierarchy of Deuteronomistic speeches that accompany the major developments recorded
in the History. Noth's omission probably has more than a little to do
with the incompatibility of the dynastic oracle with his own conception
of the purpose of the History!

Also attributed to Deuteronomistic editing, as a rule, are more
mundane features such as regnal formulae (e.g. 1 Sam. 13:1) and
archival abstracts (e.g. 1 Sam. 14:47-51), most of which are, for
obvious reasons, more characteristic of the books of Kings. Mundane
they may be, but the fact remains that the chronological framework
of the Deuteronomistic History was regarded by Noth as one of the
strongest indications of its integrity as a self-contained literary unit
(see his Chapter Four in the English translation).

Further Reading

Noth's study is now available in English translation:

> M. Noth, *The Deuteronomistic History* (*JSOT* Suppl., 15), Sheffield:
> JSOT Press, 1981 (Eng. trans. of *Überlieferungsgeschicht-*
> *liche Studien I*, 1-110, in the second edition published by
> Max Niemeyer Verlag, Tübingen, 1957).

There is a useful summary of research on the Deuteronomistic History until
about 1974 in:

> J.R. Porter, 'Old Testament Historiography', in *Tradition and*
> *Interpretation* (ed. G.W. Anderson), Oxford: Clarendon
> Press, 1979, 125-152.

For a general introduction to the content and themes of the Deuteronomistic
History see:

> J.H. Hayes, *An Introduction to Old Testament Study*, Nashville:
> Abingdon Press, 1979, 206-237.

Two studies which treat the Deuteronomistic History in the context of the
Babylonian exile are:

> P.R. Ackroyd, *Exile and Restoration. A Study of Hebrew Thought*
> *of the Sixth Century BC*, Philadelphia: Westminster /
> London: SCM Press, 1968, 62-83.

> R.W. Klein, *Israel in Exile. A Theological Interpretation*, Phila-
> delphia: Fortress Press, 1979, 23-43.

Three fairly recent studies of the Deuteronomistic History which see it as substantially a product of the Josianic period (with exilic supplementation) are:

F.M. Cross, Jr, 'The Themes of the Book of Kings and the Structure of the Deuteronomistic History', in *Canaanite Myth and Hebrew Epic. Essays in the History of the Religion of Israel*, Cambridge (Mass): Harvard University Press / London: OUP, 1973, 274-289.

R.D. Nelson, *The Double Redaction of the Deuteronomistic History* (*JSOT* Suppl., 18), Sheffield: JSOT Press, 1981.

R.E. Friedman, *The Exile and Biblical Narrative. The Formation of the Deuteronomistic and Priestly Works* (Harvard Semitic Monographs, 22), Chico: Scholars Press, 1981, 1-43.

The idea of a basic prophetic history underlying the Deuteronomistic History is considered by:

McCarter, 18-23.

Discussion of theological aspects of the Deuteronomistic History include:

G. von Rad, 'The Deuteronomistic Theology of History in the Books of Kings', in *Studies in Deuteronomy* (SBT, I/9), London: SCM Press, 1953, 74-91.

von Rad, *Old Testament Theology*, I, 334-347.

W. Brueggemann, 'The Kerygma of the Deuteronomistic Historian', *Interpretation* 22 (1968), 387-402.

H.W. Wolff, 'The Kerygma of the Deuteronomic Historical Work', in *The Vitality of Old Testament Traditions* (ed. W. Brueggemann and H.W. Wolff), Atlanta: John Knox Press, 1975, 83-100 (Eng. trans. of 'Das Kerygma des deuteronomistischen Geschichtswerks', *ZAW* 73 [1961], 171-186).

J.F.A. Sawyer, 'The Kerygma of the Deuteronomistic History', in *From Moses to Patmos. New Perspectives in Old Testament Study*, London: SPCK, 1977, 44-56.

T.N.D. Mettinger, *The Dethronement of Sabaoth. Studies in the Shem and Kabod Theologies* (Coniectanea Biblica, OT Series, 18), Lund: C.W.K. Gleerup, 1982, 38-58, 123-134.

Other important works dealing with the Deuteronomistic History are:

E.W. Nicholson, *Preaching to the Exiles. A Study of the Prose Tradition in the Book of Jeremiah*, New York: Schocken / Oxford: Blackwell, 1970, 71-93.

M. Weinfeld, *Deuteronomy and the Deuteronomic School*, Oxford: Clarendon Press, 1972.

R. Polzin, *Moses and the Deuteronomist. A Literary Study of the Deuteronomic History. Part One: Deuteronomy, Joshua, Judges*, New York: Seabury Press, 1980.

R.E. Clements, *Isaiah and the Deliverance of Jerusalem. A Study of the Interpretation of Prophecy in the Old Testament* (*JSOT* Suppl., 13), Sheffield: JSOT Press, 1980, 96-108.

Gray, 6-14, 36-43.

The following works in German should be noted:

E. Zenger, 'Die deuteronomistische Interpretation der Rehabilitierung Jojachins', *BZ* NF 12 (1968), 16-30.

L. Perlitt, *Bundestheologie im Alten Testament* (WMANT, 36), Neukirchen-Vluyn: Neukirchener Verlag, 1969, 54-128.

W. Dietrich, *Prophetie und Geschichte: Eine redaktionsgeschichtliche Untersuchung zum deuteronomistischen Geschichtswerk* (FRLANT, 108), Göttingen: Vandenhoeck & Ruprecht, 1972.

T. Veijola, *Die ewige Dynastie. David und die Entstehung seiner Dynastie nach der deuteronomistischen Darstellung*, Helsinki: Suomalainen Tiedeakatemia, 1975.

Veijola, *Das Königtum in der Beurteilung der deuteronomistischen Historiographie: eine redaktionsgeschichtliche Untersuchung*, Helsinki: Suomalainen Tiedeakatemia, 1977.

H.-D. Hoffmann, *Reform und Reformen. Untersuchungen zu einem Grundthema der deuteronomistischen Geschichtsschreibung* (ATANT, 66), Zürich: Theologischer Verlag, 1980.

See also the bibliography to chapter 4 under Birch (1976), Boecker, Crüsemann, and Weiser, and to Chapter 7 under McCarthy.

2

THE SHILOH
TRADITION

A HIGH POINT is reached in the books of Samuel when the ark of God is installed in Jerusalem and David's newly-acquired capital becomes also the 'cathedral city' of Israel (2 Sam. 6:1-19). 1 Samuel 1:1–4:1a describes the circumstances in which the sanctuary at Shiloh, which had housed the ark, forfeited that privilege because of the misdemeanours of its priesthood; so the way was opened up, and the theological justification provided, for the subsequent siting of Israel's most sacred cult object in 'David's City'. It is a skilfully-woven narrative, and scarcely patient of some of the more imaginative reconstructions of its tradition-history that have been proposed. The alternating sections on the decline of Eli's house and the ascendant star of Samuel in chs 2-3 could have existed originally as separate literary strands (cf. Hertzberg), yet even this mild conjecture puts limits on the narrative skills of the writer such as may be difficult to justify. Noth's postulation (*VT* 13 [1963], 391f.) of three separate traditions, covering Samuel's birth and dedication, the sins of Eli's family, and the call of Samuel, again suggests sensible divisions of the material without necessarily throwing light on the question of origins.

Samuel's Birth Narrative

For many scholars a special problem attaches to the story of Samuel's birth as it is told in ch. 1. When the name Samuel is given an explanation in verse 20 it is related to the Hebrew verb *šā'al* ('ask'), which word occurs several more times in chs 1-2 (1:17, 27, 28; 2:20)—always in direct speech and with reference to Samuel—and would more aptly figure in an etymology of the name Saul ('asked for'). For this reason, it is increasingly assumed that the account of Samuel's birth and dedication is a transparent remould of traditions properly belonging to the Saul cycle. I. Hylander even claimed to discover in the Samson birth narrative in Judges 13 a Danite counterpart to the Benjaminite version of Saul's birth underlying 1 Samuel 1. In his opinion both originally belonged to the Saul tradition. J. Dus, in another flight of fancy, married off Hannah, Samuel's mother, to Kish, Saul's father, and offered the information that Kish was a harsh, unloving spouse! All this, however, is to build too much on the popular etymology in 1:20, since popular etymology is often found to be at one remove from the actual significance of a name. The explanation of Samuel's name from the Hebrew verb *šā'al* is on the same level as, for example, the derivation of Babel (= Babylon) from the verb *bālal* ('confuse') in Genesis 11:9. There is the additional consideration that the occurrence of *šā'al* in 1:28—probably also in 2:20, and certainly if we follow the Qumran text—has the meaning 'lend', which is perfectly appropriate to the story of Samuel, and in particular to his mother's dedication of him to sanctuary service, but which can relate to Saul only if the birth narrative is divorced from the Shiloh tradition.

Samuel and the House of Eli

One of the most salient features of chs 2-3 is, without question, their antithetic depiction of Hannah's son and Eli's sons. Throughout the two chapters—and ch. 4 could also be included, as Willis (1972) has shown—there are alternating notices of the progress of the boy Samuel and of the ruinous career of Eli's sons, the former represented in 2:11, 18-21, 26; 3:1-10, 19–4:1a, and the latter in 2:12-17, 22-25, 27-36; 3:11-18; [4:1b-22]. The frank intention behind this structuring of the narrative is to show that Samuel was as deserving of his forthcoming preferment as were Eli's sons of their defrocking by death. Indeed, the way in which their divergent courses are described is more than a little suggestive of the later story of David and Saul, in which also the contrast is between advancement under divine auspices and demoralization without them.

The grounds for the rejection of Eli's priestly family, and therewith of the whole Shiloh cultus, are given in a speech delivered by an anonymous prophet in 2:27-36, in which the privileges of the priestly vocation are summarized and the Elide connexion is denounced for irregularities in its treatment of perquisites from sacrificial animals. It is a question not only of imminent tragedy, in the deaths of Hophni and Phinehas, but of near-annihilation (vv. 31ff.; cf. 1 Sam. 22:11-23). In the mention of a 'faithful priest' (v. 35) there is, moreover, a clear reference to Zadok as head of the Zadokite priestly family which, under Solomon, gained recognition as the sole legitimate bearers of Israelite priestly tradition, a position which they maintained for as long as the kingdom of Judah lasted. An allusion to the plight of the priests of the rural shrines who were disfranchised by Josiah's policy of centralization of worship in the Jerusalem temple is also detected in verse 36 by a number of scholars.

Hannah's Song

Locked within the prose account of the last days of Shiloh is 'Hannah's Song' (2:1-10), often categorized as a 'royal psalm', and, in any case, a distinguished representative of Hebrew psalmody, whose leading theme of the reversal of human fortunes at the intervention of God offers fitting commentary on the story of Hannah thus far. The reference to barrenness and fecundity in verse 5b strikes an especially appropriate note. While many scholars would see 'Hannah's Song' as a later element in the tradition, others have argued for its antiquity, at the least, on the basis of certain features which it shares with Canaanite and early Hebrew poetry. G.E. Wright, noting certain linguistic and thematic parallels between 'Hannah's Song' and 'The Song of Moses' in Deuteronomy 32 (principally vv. 39-42), finds the seed-bed of both in Israel's pre-monarchical holy war tradition. Following this lead, J.T. Willis (1973) connects the song of 2:1-10 with a possibly unchronicled victory by an Israelite tribe, or group of tribes, over an external enemy such as the Philistines. He then visualizes Eli and his sons teaching the victory song to the pilgrims who came to Shiloh to worship before the ark of God—among them, it is assumed, the family of Elkanah.

One difficulty that stands in the way of admitting 'Hannah's Song' into Israel's pre-monarchical psalter is the reference in its final bicolon to a king ruling under the aegis of God: 'he will give strength to his king/ and exalt the power of his anointed' (v. 10). Willis seeks to preserve the integrity of the reference in a pre-monarchical setting by limiting the original sense to local kings of the stature of Abimelech of Shechem (cf. Jdg. 9), who may have ruled during the period of the Judges. But we may seriously question whether Abimelech and his type would have been likely to inspire the utterance of 2:10b. W.F. Albright, who thought that the psalm was probably composed within the lifetime of Samuel, albeit nearer its conclusion than its beginning, did not have to exercise himself with Willis's problem, since by this stage in Samuel's life Israel had a king. Even so, Albright changes the vowels of the Hebrew *malkô*, 'his king', to *molkô*, 'his [i.e. God's] reign', claiming that the root *mlk* often means 'kingdom, reign' in the Old Testament, as well as in the related dialects of Ugaritic and Phoenician. Since, nevertheless, the next line speaks of God's 'anointed', it seems hardly possible to evacuate the verse of all reference to an earthly, in this instance Israelite, ruler, and Albright rightly refrains. Gottwald, who views the psalm as a product of 'the premonarchic egalitarian community of Israel', takes verse 10b as a later addition.

However, uncertainty about the origin of the references to 'king' and 'anointed' in 2:10b should not obscure the fact that within the larger context of 1 and 2 Samuel they are intended to express the Davidic kingship ideology, according to which the Davidic king is both 'God's king' and 'God's anointed'. At the other end of the books of Samuel the 'Psalm of David', which celebrates the king's deliverance from his enemies, and which echoes some of the expressions in 'Hannah's Song', finishes on the same note: 'Great triumphs he gives to his king / and shows steadfast love to his anointed / to David, and his descendants for ever' (2 Sam. 22:51). The 'anointed' of 2:10b is, then, the same as 'my anointed' in verse 35 later in the chapter, where it is unquestionably the Davidic king, presiding over the Zadokite priesthood, who is in view. This adumbration of the Davidic king already in 'Hannah's Song' well befits a book which, according to one line of tradition, as we have seen, was counted as the first of four 'Books of Reigns'. It is also the appropriate clef sign for the story of Samuel, one of whose chief claims to fame from the standpoint of later history was, as the proportions of 1 Samuel suggest, his role as king-maker—first in relation to Saul, it is true, but pre-eminently in relation to David.

Samuel the Prophet

In chs 1-3 the main lines of Samuel's career are established. He is depicted as, to a point, the heir to the functions and authority exercised by the Elide priesthood, but with the major difference that, at a time when vision and oracles were rare (3:1), he was possessed of prophetic insight and enjoyed that authentication of his utterances which, according to Deuteronomy 18:22, was the proof of a prophet. It was principally as a prophet that Samuel's memory was preserved in the tradition, so much so that as an exponent of prophetic intercession he takes his place in later literature alongside Moses (Jer. 15:1; cf. Ps. 99:6). Since the prophets claimed to speak in the name of God, the question 'By what authority?' was a lively one and, in the Old Testament, is partly answered in the 'prophetic call narrative'. The narrative of Samuel's call is in 3:1-14 and is in the form of an 'audition', or interview with Yahweh, in which he learns of the destruction of Eli's priestly house. While, then, the narrative has its own peculiar features, it is representative of the genre to the extent that the fledgeling prophet is entrusted with a message of judgment which he would almost certainly not have chosen to hear (cf. Jer. 1:4ff.).

The circumstances of the times and the strength of his own personality will have been two decisive factors in the role-casting of Samuel; at a later stage in Israel's history, in an era of specialization, it would not have been possible for an individual to combine the offices of prophet, priest, and judge-administrator as Samuel appears to have done.

1 Samuel 1-7

In spite of the widespread tendency to regard 4:1b–7:1 as a distinct literary entity (see next section), Willis (1971) argues that it is wrong to dissever chs 1-7 in this way, partly because 4:1b–7:1 presupposes information given in chs 1-3, and partly because of certain narrative features, such as the references to Eli's blindness, which straddle the supposed dividing-line. Willis therefore treats chs 1-7 as a unit and attributes its composition to disciples of Samuel living in Ramah. The view propounded by Dus, that chs 1-3 were compiled in the early years of Solomon's reign by a member of the Zadokite priesthood in order to serve as an introduction to the 'Ark Narrative' would go some way to meeting Willis's points, but, like all attempts to determine the date and provenance of this section, must remain hypothetical.

An observation of more general import may be made here, namely that traditions transmitted at a particular sanctuary or among a particular coterie were not necessarily maintained in hermetic isolation from traditions preserved elsewhere. It should not surprise us, therefore, if independent sources purporting to represent related sets of circumstances are actually found to agree on points of detail. Our position on this matter will also depend on how we regard such a reference as 4:4b, which, in an independent 'Ark Narrative', could be read as a matter-of-fact comment about the tending of the ark when it was taken to the battle-front, or which could, in its present setting, hint at approaching disaster.

Further Reading

For historical background and reconstruction see:

W.F. Albright, *Samuel and the Beginnings of the Prophetic Movement*, Cincinnati: Hebrew Union College, 1961.

The following article discusses 1 Samuel 1-7 as a single narrative complex:

J.T. Willis, 'An Anti-Elide Narrative Tradition from a Prophetic Circle at the Ramah Sanctuary', *JBL* 90 (1971), 288-308.

On the Samuel birth story see:

J.T. Willis, 'Cultic Elements in the Story of Samuel's Birth and Dedication', *STh* 26 (1972), 33-61.

The following studies in German are also noteworthy:

I. Hylander, *Der literarische Samuel—Saul—Komplex (I. Sam. 1-15) traditionsgeschichtlich untersucht*, Uppsala: Almqvist & Wiksell, 1932, 9-62.

J. Dus, 'Die Geburtslegende Samuels, I. Sam. 1 (Eine traditionsgeschichtliche Untersuchung zu I. Sam. 1-3)', *RSO* 43 (1968), 163-194.

On 'Hannah's Song' see:

G.E. Wright, 'The Lawsuit of God: A Form-Critical Study of Deuteronomy 32', in *Israel's Prophetic Heritage* (Festschrift J. Muilenburg; ed. B.W. Anderson, W. Harrelson), London: SCM Press, 1962, 57f.

W.F. Albright, *Yahweh and the Gods of Canaan*, London: Athlone Press, 1968, 18f.

J.T. Willis, 'The Song of Hannah and Psalm 113', *CBQ* 35 (1973), 139-154.

N.K. Gottwald, *The Tribes of Yahweh. A Sociology of the Religion of Liberated Israel, 1250-1050 B.C.E.*, London: SCM Press, 1980, 534-540.

For discussion of Samuel's call in the context of Israelite prophecy see:

M. Newman, 'The Prophetic Call of Samuel', in *Israel's Prophetic Heritage* (see above), 86-97.

On the prophetic call in more general terms see:

G. von Rad, *The Message of the Prophets*, New York: Harper & Row / London: SCM Press, 1968, 30-49.

For a recent evaluation of 1 Samuel 3 in terms of a near eastern dream theophany see:

R. Gnuse, 'A Reconsideration of the Form-Critical Structure in I Samuel 3: An Ancient Near Eastern Dream Theophany', *ZAW* 94 (1982), 379-390.

3

THE ARK
NARRATIVE

1. Definition

T HE ENTHUSIASTIC appraisal of Samuel as 'a prophet of the
LORD' in 3:19–4:1a is immediately followed by a detailed report
of a national disaster from which he is a conspicuous absentee. Neither
in the preliminaries to the battles with the Philistines at Ebenezer, nor
in the arrangements for the deposition of the ark at Kiriath-jearim, is
any role ascribed to Samuel. The explanation that chs 4-6 describe
events from that period when he was still the acolyte of Shiloh may
take care of the historical problem, but there still remains the literary
problem of 3:19–4:1a, in which he appears already as an established
prophet of national importance. Considerations of this sort have
inclined the majority of recent scholars, following an earlier lead by
Leonhard Rost, to regard chs 4-6, with the possible addition of 2
Samuel 6, as representing an originally self-contained 'Ark Narrative'
which rehearsed the fortunes of this sacred cult object from its
introduction to the battle-front at Ebenezer to its return to Israelite
territory and—if 2 Samuel 6 be included—its installation in David's
new capital. If there is substance to the theory, then we may better
understand the 'strange silences' of chs 4-6, whether on the role of
Samuel or the fate of Shiloh. But, 'Ark Narrative' or no, it remains the
case that all else in these chapters is subordinated to the glorification of
the ark as the abode of a divine power which, once freed from the
shackles of disobedient Israel, works havoc among the enemies of
Yahweh.

Rost believed that the Ark Narrative was the *hieros logos* ('cult
myth') for the Jerusalem temple where the ark was finally housed—an
account of the previous history of the ark intended for the edification
of festival pilgrims when they came to Jerusalem. Because of certain

priestly interests reflected in the narrative, for example, the naming of the several custodians of the ark in an account in which names are sparse, Rost attributed its authorship to a priest active in David's reign, or perhaps early in Solomon's.

Three fairly recent monographs have continued the Rost tradition to the extent that they each acknowledge a discrete literary entity identifiable with the Ark Narrative. A.F. Campbell's conclusions most nearly agree with Rost's, both as to the delimitation of the source boundaries and in his dating of the Narrative to the tenth century. But the category of festal legend does not come into Campbell's definition; rather, the Narrative is essentially a theological reflection on the end of an epoch within Israel's history. It offers, says Campbell, no explanation of God's temporary repudiation of Israel—just the affirmation that the nation's trauma is God's doing. And in the same way, that new era that is heralded by the installation of the ark in Jerusalem (2 Sam. 6) is shown to have come about under divine auspices.

A different era and another set of preoccupations are envisaged in F. Schicklberger's study of the ark in 1 Samuel. Here several lines of investigation converge on the reign of Hezekiah as the period when an Ark Narrative consisting of most of 1 Samuel 5-6 was wedded to an older 'catastrophe-account' comprising some elements of ch. 4. Schicklberger sees ch. 5 as a polemic against the cult of the Assyrian plague-god Nergal-Resheph, which had been gaining adherents in the northern kingdom. Now, in a time of crisis for Judah following the Assyrians' subjugation of the north, the author of the Narrative wanted to stress God's continuing association with the ark. Several arguments against the inclusion of 2 Samuel 6 in the Narrative are pressed by Schicklberger. Some are easily disposed of, and have been suitably answered by Campbell (1979) in an economically-worded response which also takes account of the monograph by Miller and Roberts (see below). Schicklberger's characterization of 2 Samuel 6 as more history-like than 1 Samuel 4-6, for example, is justly stigmatized as being too subjective. Furthermore, it is only by dint of having separated 1 Samuel 4 from 1 Samuel 5-6 that Schicklberger can sustain his claim that 2 Samuel 6 deals with definite, named individuals in a way that sets it apart from his version of the Ark Narrative. Again, the distinction between the 'active' ark of 1 Samuel 5-6 and the 'passive' ark of 2 Samuel 6 depends on the dismissal of the Perez-uzzah incident in the latter passage as aetiological *and* secondary.

Miller and Roberts, in the most recent monograph on the Ark

Narrative, side with Schicklberger over the status of 2 Samuel 6. They are, however, more interested in determining the starting-point of the Narrative in 1 Samuel. In their opinion, 4:1b is an unsatisfactory beginning because it means that Eli and his sons make their appearance (v. 4) without any word of introduction or explanation. A second difficulty is that the Narrative, as hitherto conceived, suggests no reason for the judgments that are visited on Israel. As to the first point, it may be that Eli and his family, like so many visiting speakers, were reckoned to 'need no introduction'; Schicklberger's suggestion that the audience were Shilonites is also meant to take care of this point. In remedy of the second, and more serious, deficiency, Miller and Roberts prefix the anti-Elide portions of ch. 2 (vv. 12-17, 22-25, 27-36) to ch. 4, so that, even in the Ark Narrative, it becomes clear that the disasters of ch. 4 are in retribution for the sins of the house of Eli. However, while this is the undoubted implication of the text in its present arrangement, it does not automatically follow that, in an independent Ark Narrative, the nexus of sin and judgment would have been nearly so important. If glorification of the ark was the *raison d'être* of the account, we need no more assume that it proffered an explanation for Israel's ills than that it described the consequences for Shiloh. It is true that Miller and Roberts prefer to speak of a 'Yahweh Narrative' instead of an 'Ark Narrative', on the ground that the issue is 'not what happens to the ark, but what Yahweh is doing among his people'; but a more accurate summary of these chapters would speak of God's activity in conjunction with the ark—and not only among the Israelites, for approximately half of the Narrative is concerned with the ark's sojourn in Philistia.

One of the most keenly-felt difficulties with Rost's delimitation of the Ark Narrative is the variation in names as between 1 Samuel 7:1 and 2 Samuel 6:2ff. In the former the location of the ark after its return from Philistia is given as Kiriath-jearim, whereas in the latter it is said to have been Baale-Judah. Now, by the simple expedient of cross-referring to Joshua 15:9 we may conclude that these are alternative names for the same place. However, while the verisimilitude of the story is not much affected, the existence of such variants in what would originally have been contiguous verses might be regarded as improbable. Campbell's answer is to treat Baale-Judah, not as a place-name, but as two separate words meaning 'the citizens of Judah'; this is, however, a questionable procedure. In the first instance, this use of the Hebrew *ba'al* is unparalleled in the Old Testament; with dubious exception, when the word means 'citizen' it is linked with a city (cf.

Jdg. 9, *passim*). Secondly, Campbell's translation requires auxiliary hypotheses for its justification, in particular the treatment of verse 1 as a dislodged introduction to the summary of David's military achievements in 2 Samuel 8. Otherwise 'from there' (v. 2) is a trifle remote from its supposed antecedent (Kiriath-jearim, 1 Sam. 7:2). However, the Assyrian text cited by Miller and Roberts (pp. 15f.) in their discussion of 2 Samuel 6 shows that a large military display on the occasion of the installation of the ark would have been entirely appropriate. The corroborative evidence of 1 Chronicles 13:1; 15:25 is valuable in this regard, because the Chronicler is not simply reproducing the standard (Massoretic) text of Samuel at these points. Finally, at 2 Samuel 6:2 the Qumran text has 'Baalah', which is unquestionably a proper name.

The variant names given in 1 Samuel 7:1 and 2 Samuel 6:3 for the sons of Abinadab who took charge of the ark are less of an obstacle to the inclusion of 2 Samuel 6 in the Narrative. Perhaps nothing more than the elapse of time is necessary to explain the difference. But, not content with this, Campbell prefers to vocalize *'ḥyw* in 2 Samuel 6:3f. as a suffixed noun ('his brother'), rather than as a proper name. However, even when allowance is made for the fact that the narrative is about to describe the mysterious death of Uzzah, it is strange to find the other custodian of the ark being twice referred to anonymously as 'his brother', particularly since, in the second occurrence (v. 4), the suffix would lack a proper antecedent.

In his rejoinder article noted above, Campbell appeals to the inner dynamic of the Narrative in support of his contention that 2 Samuel 6 is its proper conclusion. Without this chapter, he argues, the ark remains at a distance from any acknowledged sanctuary in Israel; is this a likely conclusion to the story of the ark's 'exile and restoration'? It is a fair point, yet it must be conceded that stories have had worse endings than 1 Samuel 7:1, and that the consecration of Eleazar to the service of the ark is a satisfactory resolution of a crisis which began with the sacred box suffering the ministrations of Eli's sons (1 Sam. 4:4). Since even total narrative coherence between 1 Samuel 4–6 and 2 Samuel 6 would be no guarantee of a common origin in a single source, it may be that the issue should turn on a relatively small matter such as the variation in place-names, as between 1 Samuel 7:1 and 2 Samuel 6:2, discussed above.

It will be evident from the foregoing discussion that the lineaments of the 'Ark Narrative', if it ever existed, have yet to be restored with a

proper degree of exactitude. Since, however, 1 Samuel 4–6 forms what
is, by any reasonable criterion, a coherent unit of tradition, the
following discussion of theme should retain its value regardless of the
source-critical question.

2. Theme

The background to the Israelites' double discomfiture at Ebenezer is
the struggle for *Lebensraum* which was waged between the Israelites
and the Philistines in the early Iron Age, and which erupted in
episodic fits until David's comprehensive victories in the Rephaim
valley (2 Sam. 5:17-25). In the same general period when the
Israelites were pressing their territorial claims in Canaan, the
Philistines, recent arrivals from the Mediterranean area, were establishing their hold on the coastal belt to the west of the Shephelah
lowlands. (It is noteworthy, then, that the prophet Amos, when
taking issue with those who put too much store by Israel's election
traditions, links the 'exoduses' of the Israelites and the Philistines as
being equally facets of God's activity among the nations [9:7].)
Egyptian texts from the reign of Rameses III (early twelfth century)
mention various peoples, including the *Prst* (i.e. Philistines), who
arrived at the frontiers of Egypt in an unavailing attempt to settle
there. These formed part of the great migration of 'Sea Peoples'
which swept into the Fertile Crescent at the end of the Bronze Age,
with devastating effect on some once-powerful states in the area.
Rameses' temple inscriptions at Medinet Habu recount, with relish
and hyperbole, the defeats inflicted on those members of the confeder-
ation who tried to enter Egypt. Some of the assailants, and notably
the Philistines, were diverted into south-west Canaan, where they
settled in the coastal strip south of the plain of Sharon—hence (via
the Greek historian Herodotus) the name 'Palestine' for this general
region. The flag-carriers of the Philistine occupation were the five
cities of the 'Philistine pentapolis', as it tends to be known: Ashdod,
Ashkelon, Ekron, Gath, and Gaza (cf. 1 Sam. 6:17).

Seen from an Old Testament perspective, the struggle between the
Israelites and the Philistines revolved around two basic issues. In the
first place, the Philistines' presence in Canaan seemed to challenge
Israel's right to occupy land that was the subject of ancient promises
to the fathers. Secondly, the two contestants represented two compet-
ing, and incompatible, religious ideologies. In the socio-religious
sphere the Philistines of the Old Testament could be said to stand for

acculturation and assimilation. For example, there are but very frugal remains of the original Philistine language, presumably because they quickly adopted the Canaanite dialect of the people among whom they settled. There is certainly no consciousness of a language barrier between Hebrews and Philistines in the various Old Testament stories involving Philistines. Again, Egyptian-type anthropoid coffins found on several sites associated with the Philistines or their allies — most recently at Deir el-Balaḥ, south-west of Gaza—illustrate their capacity for adjusting to the customs and practices of those with whom they came into contact. However, the mimetic tendencies of the Philistines are most apparent in the ideologically sensitive area of religious devotion and practice: the only deities with which they are associated in the Old Testament, viz. Dagon, Ashtoreth, and Beelzebub, are members of the Semitic pantheon. It is for this kind of reason that the Philistines represent something more than mere military opposition in certain parts of the Hebrew Bible. (The contemptuous references to 'uncircumcised Philistines', on the other hand, show that these 'westerners' had resisted at least one practice that was widespread in the near east [cf. Jer. 9:25f.].)

Israel's vocation was formulated in terms precisely the opposite of what we have said about the Philistines. 'Tear down their altars' and 'break their pillars' (Exod. 34:13) are given as the marching orders of the Israelites prior to their departure from Sinai for Canaan. Much, therefore, that Israel was forbidden to do, and that the classical prophets would later denounce in the cultic realm, seems to have been second nature to the Philistines. History would show that it was second nature for all too many Israelites, but that was in spite of every encouragement to do better.

In 1 Samuel 4–6 the two ideologies meet in representative combat, not on the battlefield of Ebenezer, but right in the heart of Philistia, and most famously in the temple of Dagon. The contest is not between Israel and Philistia, but between Israel's God and the gods of the Philistines. In this regard, as also in the shared plague motif, these chapters recall the Exodus story—which is never far from the narrator's mind, to judge from the allusions and echoes which pervade his account. The motivation is the same: 'on all the gods of Egypt (or 'Philistia') I will execute judgments' (Exod. 12:12), and so, in the cities of Philistia, Israel's God shows himself again as 'a man of war' (cf. Exod. 15:3), wreaking havoc wherever the 'captured' ark is taken, in a veritable parody of a victory tour.

Before that, however, there was the decisive confrontation with
Dagon. It was customary for victorious armies in the near east to
remove the 'defeated' gods from their temples and install them in the
temples of their own gods, and the practice illuminates 1 Samuel 5:1-
5. But, as the Philistines will have discovered at one time or another,
the Israelites' God was worshipped without images ('the aniconic
God'); on this occasion, therefore, they take a functional equivalent
of an image, viz. the ark of the covenant. (In the exilic period the
'vessels of the house of the LORD' would fulfil a similar function [cf.
Ezra 1:8ff., etc.].) The ark is brought to Ashdod and placed in the
presence of Dagon, supposedly the victorious god, and, all unbeknown
to the Philistines, the scene is set for the contest proper to begin. The
judgment on Dagon as the representative god of Philistia happens at
night (cf. Exod. 12:12), and is in two stages, as if to correspond to the
twin defeats of Israel at Ebenezer. Now, in a striking reversal of roles,
Dagon is prostrated before the ark, a hapless torso. Hereafter there is
no talk of the gods of Philistia; even Philistine priests are made to
speak like Hebrew prophets (6:6).

Miller and Roberts find the Ark Narrative to be 'one of the oldest
and most profound theological narratives of the Old Testament'
(p. 60), and, without prejudice to the question of dating, we may
certainly agree with this assessment of the contents. For here is an
impressive assertion of the power of the God of Israel, who does not
go into eclipse with his people, but who may even, if he chooses, use
their calamities as the foil for his mightiest acts. That was an insight
filled with hope for the various crises in Israel's history and, most
poignantly of all, for the night of exile when that history seemed to
have been given its quietus. The Ark Narrative has a word—
literally—for this eventuality; it is the verb *gālāh*, translatable as
'depart', but in almost all its occurrences meaning 'go into exile', and
it is used in 4:21f.: 'the glory has departed (has been exiled?) from
Israel'. It was in roughly comparable terms that the prophet Ezekiel
in the early sixth century BC depicted the abandonment by God of
his sanctuary—a reluctant withdrawal of the divine glory, heralding
the destruction of Jerusalem and Judah (Ezek. 9:3; 10:4, 18f.;
11:22f.). But just as the story of the ark is of *temporary* exile, of a God
who cannot be subjugated even when his people are overwhelmed
and his sacred casket is in enemy hands, so to the generation of the
exile may it not have been parabolic of what God could yet do with
the friable, even now broken, community of Israel? In our ignorance

of the fate of the ark in 587 BC—despite 2 Maccabees 2 and the tradition that Jeremiah hid it in a cave!—we can but assume that, even if it was destroyed, there were those who could extrapolate on the message of 1 Samuel 4-6 so as to anticipate that the glory would return. It did in Ezekiel's vision of the rebuilt temple (Ezek. 43:1-5; 44:4), and it was the lively hope of the post-exilic prophets Haggai (2:7, 9) and Zechariah (2:5).

Further Reading

Rost's influential study has recently been translated into English:

L. Rost, *The Succession to the Throne of David* (Historic Texts and Interpreters in Biblical Scholarship, 1), Sheffield: Almond Press, 1982, 6-34 (= *Die Überlieferung von der Thronnachfolge Davids* (BWANT III.6 [= 42]), Stuttgart: Kohlhammer, 1926).

Two important monographs published in English in the past decade are:

A.F. Campbell, *The Ark Narrative (1 Sam. 4-6; 2 Sam. 6). A Form-critical and Traditio-historical Study* (SBL Dissertation Series, 16), Missoula: SBL and Scholars Press, 1975.

P.D. Miller, Jr and J.J.M. Roberts, *The Hand of the Lord. A Reassessment of the 'Ark Narrative' of 1 Samuel*, Baltimore/London: Johns Hopkins University Press, 1977.

McCarter, 23-26, follows Miller and Roberts closely.

The third monograph is in German:

F. Schicklberger, *Die Ladeerzählungen des ersten Samuel-Buches. Eine literaturwissenschaftliche und theologiegeschichtliche Untersuchung* (Forschung zur Bibel, 7), Würzburg: Echter Verlag, 1973.

Note also the following two articles, the second sceptical about the separate existence of the Ark Narrative:

A.F. Campbell, 'Yahweh and the Ark: A Case Study in Narrative', *JBL* 98 (1979), 31-43.

J.T. Willis, 'Samuel Versus Eli, I Sam. 1-7', *TZ* 35 (1979), 201-212.

The following article in German considers the possible function of the Ark Narrative in the historical context of the Babylonian exile:

H. Timm, 'Die Ladeerzählung (1. Sam. 4-6; 2. Sam. 6) und das Kerygma des deuteronomistischen Geschichtswerks', *EvTh* 26 (1966), 509-526.

The history of the 'ark of the covenant' is discussed in the following:

R.E. Clements, *God and Temple*, Oxford: Blackwell, 1965, 28-39.

M.H. Woudstra, *The Ark of the Covenant from Conquest to Kingship*, Philadelphia: Presbyterian and Reformed Publishing Company, 1965.

G. Henton Davies, 'The Ark of the Covenant', *ASTI* 5 (1966-7), 30-47.

P.R. Davies, 'The History of the Ark in the Books of Samuel', *JNSL* 5 (1977), 9-18.

For discussion of the verbal and ideological parallels between the Ark Narrative and the Exodus tradition see:

D. Daube, *The Exodus Pattern in the Bible*, Westport, Ct: Greenwood Press / London: Faber and Faber, 1963, 73-88.

The issue as to whether Shiloh was destroyed in the aftermath of the second battle described in 1 Samuel 4 is treated by:

J. Day, 'The Destruction of the Shiloh Sanctuary and Jeremiah VII 12, 14', *VTS* 30 (1979), 87-94.

The following studies give attention to the near eastern ideology reflected in the Ark Narrative:

M. Delcor, 'Jahweh et Dagon, ou le Jahwisme face à la religion des Philistins, d'après 1 Sam. V', *VT* 14 (1964), 136-154 (reprinted in *Etudes bibliques et orientales de religions comparées*, Leiden: Brill, 1979, 30-48).

Campbell (1975), 179-191.

Miller and Roberts, 9-17, 76-87.

Relevant material from the Neo-Assyrian period is discussed in:

M. Cogan, *Imperialism and Religion: Assyria, Judah and Israel in the Eighth and Seventh Centuries B.C.E.* (SBL Monograph Series, 19), Missoula: Scholars Press, 1974, 9-41.

Information on the Philistines may be found in:

T.C. Mitchell, 'Philistia', in *AOTS*, 405-427.

E.E. Hindson, *The Philistines and the Old Testament*, Grand Rapids: Baker, 1972.

K.A. Kitchen, 'The Philistines', in *POTT*, 53-78.

N.K. Sandars, *The Sea Peoples. Warriors of the ancient Mediterranean, 1250-1150 BC*, London: Thames and Hudson, 1978, 164-170.

T. Dothan, *The Philistines and their Material Culture*, New Haven/London: Yale University Press, 1982.

Gottwald, 410-425 (see bibliography to Chapter 2).

4

THE RISE OF
THE MONARCHY

IT IS WITH the rise of the monarchy that we can truly speak of
Israel as a nation, and the importance of the development is
reflected in the space given to it in 1 Samuel. Moreover, since, in the
opinion of the Hebrew historians, the respective monarchies of Judah
and Israel contributed generously to the undoing of those states, the
account of the beginnings assumed still greater importance, as partly
providing the explanation of the unprosperous course of the kingdoms
between the tenth and sixth centuries BC. In 1 Samuel 7-12,
therefore, we are made aware, not only of the contrary evaluations of
the institution as they will have been current at the end of the
eleventh century, but also of the debate which continued to be waged
as the flawed nature of the monarchy became ever more apparent.

The story of Saul's emergence as Israel's first king proceeds by a
number of stages which may be summarized as: (i) a request for a
king by the tribal elders of Israel (8:1-22); (ii) the private anointing of
Saul (9:1–10:16); (iii) divine nomination and public presentation
(10:17-27); (iv) military success and public acclamation (11:1-15); (v)
final speech by Samuel (12:1-25). On stylistic and other grounds it
seems likely that different sources or traditions have been combined
to form the present neatly-structured narrative. From the time of
Julius Wellhausen it has been traditional to divide the five main
sections according as they display a favourable or an unfavourable
attitude towards the monarchy. By this method of reckoning 9:1–
10:16 and 11:1-15 are classified as 'favourable', while 8:1-22, 10:17-27,
and 12:1-25 are regarded as 'unfavourable'. A regularly-entertained
corollary is that the pro-monarchical passages are earlier than the
others, with 11:1-15 corresponding most nearly of all to the circum-

stances in which Saul came to the throne. But so far we have said nothing about ch. 7, and it is there that we must begin our review of contents.

1 Samuel 7:2-17

The fact that chs 8-12 appear to form a discrete entity dealing with the inauguration of the monarchy should not blind us to the importance of ch. 7 in relation to this same theme. This chapter mentions neither king nor monarchy, it is true, and yet it represents a point of view as much as any of the five 'tableaux' listed above. It is when the chapter is read as a preface to chs 8-12, and not in isolation, that its purpose becomes clear. The background is Israel's subservience to their Philistine rivals and the ever-present threat of further indignities from hostile neighbours—a threat which runs through chs 8-12 as well (cf. 8:20; 9:16; 10:1[LXX], 27; 11:1-15; 12:12), and which was largely responsible for driving the Israelites to the political expedient of monarchy. At a national convention at Mizpah, as ch. 7 recounts, the people of Israel were challenged by Samuel to renounce their pagan ways and serve the God of Israel, trusting in him for deliverance from the Philistines. Paradoxically, this very convocation attracted the attention of the enemy, who thereupon massed for attack. Contrary to the expectations of both sides, the Philistines were routed and expelled altogether from Israelite territory (vv. 13f.), thanks to the decisive intervention of Israel's God.

Since there is an idealized presentation of events and their consequences here (for example, compare v. 13 with 9:16, 10:5, and chs 13-14), our concern should be less with questions of historical reconstruction and more with the theological function of the chapter, which is to show that the old theocracy of the period of the Judges was as capable of dealing with Israel's military emergencies as of directing its social and religious life. With this in mind we can discover more than a merely topographical significance in the explanation of the name 'Ebenezer' given to the stone which commemorated the victory (v. 12). 'To this point the LORD helped us' may have either a local or a temporal significance, and, while the former is certainly possible (i.e. 'the rout extended this far, with God's help'), a temporal meaning would convey most effectively the general point that the chapter is making: 'we have succeeded thus far in our history because God has been with us'. The unspoken

suggestion is that it has been done without a king, and that there is no
need of one, now or ever. So also in the summary of Israel's military
achievements during Samuel's lifetime we are informed, not only of
the recovery of lost territory, but also of internal stability as reflected
in the good relations between Israel and the Amorites, who are here
representative of the pre-Israelite population of Canaan that had
survived the conquest (vv. 13f.). In short, the conclusive victory and
the large claims built upon it are intended to leave Israel without
excuse as, through the representation of the elders, they petition
Samuel (see ch. 8) for a king to govern them and to lead them in
battle.

1 Samuel 8:1-22

Samuel's response to this request is hostile, consisting in the main of
an unflattering word portrait of the king whom they seek: he will be a
despot who, by his exactions from his subjects, will turn them into
slaves (8:11-18). The characteristic action of their king will be to
'take'—both people and possessions—until the grossness of the error
of appointing a king will be obvious to all. Because of the measure of
correspondence between this sketch and certain aspects of the reign
of Solomon as described in 1 Kings, it has often been assumed that
Samuel's speech draws inspiration from the despotic record of that
monarch, or, perhaps, of certain of his successors who followed his
'kingly' ways and are now presented in composite portrait. The
'Solomonic' view has enjoyed vigorous advocacy in Clements's 1974
essay, in which he argues that the Deuteronomistic historian's
criticisms of Solomon, muted in 1 Kings because of his desire to
brand Jeroboam I as the chief of royal sinners, have been transferred
to 1 Samuel 8, where they perform the more useful task of denigrating
Saul. When, therefore, Samuel warns of a day when the people of
Israel will 'cry out' for relief from subservience to their king (8:18), it
is the council of Shechem (1 Kgs 12) that is in view. Again, noting the
Deuteronomistic tendency to censure kings for failure in the religio-
cultic realm, Clements concludes that 1 Samuel 8:11-18, with its
emphasis on social and administrative abuses, must originally have
been a pre-Deuteronomistic formulation.

'Pre-Deuteronomistic' would be an understatement as far as
I. Mendelsohn's view of Samuel's speech is concerned. Mendelsohn,
having matched the speech against the outline of kingship (Canaanite-

style) which emerges from Akkadian texts recovered at Ras Shamra (ancient Ugarit), decided that it reflected, not the aberrations of the Israelite monarchy from Solomon onwards, but the common practice of the kings and kinglets of the Canaanite city-states with which Samuel and his contemporaries would have been acquainted. Mendelsohn's little study, published in 1956, has been quite influential in subsequent discussions of 1 Samuel 8. In his insistence on an early date of origin for the king-portrait he has found a recent ally in F. Crüsemann, who traces it back to the period of the early monarchy. Crüsemann finds a community of interest between Samuel's speech and the dissatisfaction which fuelled the rebellions by Absalom and Sheba already in David's reign. It is also important for Crüsemann that the anti-monarchical outbursts in Hosea mark, not the beginning of a trend, but its mid-point.

As to the specific linking of 1 Samuel 8:11-18 with the reign of Solomon, the arguments are not convincing. For, although the general tenor of the speech may be compatible with what we know of Solomon's administration, it is noteworthy that the gravamen of the popular case against Solomon, viz. his conscription of fellow-Israelites to work on his building projects, remains unexpressed in these verses. On the other hand, the description of the corvée (forced labour) arrangements in 1 Kings 5:13-18, the rise to prominence of Jeroboam, whom Solomon had put in charge of the levy of 'the house of Joseph' (1 Kgs 11:28; 12:1ff.), and the stoning of Adoniram (1 Kgs 12:18; cf. 5:14), all witness to the importance of this feature of Solomon's administration. So too do the catchwords in the northerners' complaint at the Shechem parley: 'hard service' and 'yoke', 'chastise' and 'whips' (1 Kgs 12:4, 11). But of building programmes and labour-gangs there is not a hint in Samuel's speech; whereas what we might have expected in a profile of Solomon, even of Solomon incognito, is something of the order of, 'And he will make you stonecutters and carriers'. Such a reference would be no more of an 'anachronism' in 1 Samuel 8 than are the horses and chariots of verses 11f.

A further argument against taking 1 Samuel 8:11-18 as the debit side of Solomon's reign is the fact that similar policies are associated with other kings of Israel, Saul included. For the latter we have 1 Samuel 22:7 ('Will the son of Jesse give every one of you fields and vineyards, will he make you all commanders of thousands and commanders of hundreds . . . ?'), and it is unnecessary to treat this as an editorial invention calculated to bring Saul under Samuel's condemnation. In bestowing favours on his kinsmen Saul would have been doing only what was natural, not to say politically expedient. His appointment of his cousin Abner as his commander-in-chief is a case in point; David's promotion of Joab and Abishai similarly combined nepotism and good sense. As for Saul's acquisition of livestock, and of servants to tend them, the almost incidental reference to the Edomite Doeg as 'the chief of Saul's herdsmen' (1 Sam. 21:7 RSV) might afford illustration, were it not for some uncertainty about the word translated 'herdsmen'. Finally, there is the observation in 1 Samuel 14:52, at the conclusion of a section wholly laudatory of Saul (vv. 47ff.), that 'whenever Saul saw a mighty or a brave man, he took him into his service'. It has even been suggested that this policy may have given rise to a rudimentary system of taxation before ever David and Solomon appeared on the scene. Just as unpopular, in any case, would have been the expropriations necessary to provide fiefs for his serving kinsmen. It is to be concluded, therefore, that the description of kingly acquisitiveness in Samuel's speech is not specially applicable to Solomon's reign, since what is given is nothing more than a general sketch of the ways of kings in and out of Israel, and in almost any period.

1 Samuel 9:1–10:16

At 9:1 we encounter a different atmosphere, a difference made all the more noticeable by the absence of a formal literary bridge with the preceding narrative. The story-line has a folkloristic complexion, recounting how a young man went in search of his father's lost asses and serendipitously acquired a kingdom for himself. The outright classification of 9:1–10:16 as 'folklore', as advocated by some scholars, is based partly on the improbable ease with which event follows event as Saul is conducted towards his moment of destiny. But it is doubtful whether this does full justice to the narrative's stress on the providential ordering of circumstances, not only as bringing Saul to the throne, but also as proclaiming him to be God's own choice as king.

A notable feature of the narrative in its early stages is its low-key presentation of Samuel, who is unknown to Saul, as it would appear, yet is of sufficient standing for Saul's servant to have heard of him. What, we ask, has happened to the grand old prophet known and respected 'from Dan to Beersheba'? It is not surprising that literary criticism has been called in to deal with the problem, nor is it unreasonable to think of separate traditions woven together so as to be now indistinguishable by literary-critical methods (cf. Hertzberg). (Usually the supposition is that later elements relating to Samuel's anointing of Saul have been superimposed on an old account of Saul's meeting with an anonymous local seer.) But it could be that the explanation lies elsewhere. Is it possible that Saul's ignorance and Samuel's inconspicuousness are literary devices to create suspense and to invest the proceedings with a sense of mystery appropriate to the lofty business of appointing Israel's first king? From this point of view Samuel's announcement, 'I am the seer' (9:19), would be a high point in the story, rather than primarily a literary transition from one source to another. Saul's ignorance of Samuel's existence would then function, by a kind of metonymy, for his ignorance of God's plans for him in relation to the throne. There are two other points which suggest that there is more to Saul's ignorance than immediately meets the eye. First, if Curtis (*VT* 29 (1979), 491-493) is right in detecting a folk etymology of the Hebrew word for 'prophet' (*nābî'*) in Saul's question, 'What shall we bring (*mah-nnābî'*)?', in 9:7—i.e. a prophet is someone to whom you *bring* something—then not just the explanatory note in 9:9 but the whole of 9:5-10 is concerned with the nomenclature of prophecy. In that case the appeal to an old seer tradition as the explanation of Saul's ignorance would be beside the point. Secondly, we may wonder whether the servant's comment about the seer's words coming true (v. 6) does not deliberately echo what is said of Samuel in 3:19: 'and the LORD was with him and let none of his words fall to the ground' ('comes true' in 9:6 recalls Dt. 18:22 and the test of genuine prophecy).

While there is nothing in 9:1–10:16 that is overtly anti-monarchical, clarity is not served by labelling the section pro-monarchical, for no further objection to the idea of kingship is to be expected here in the light of the concession granted in 8:22. Moreover, the grounds for caution are strengthened when we note the solitary occurrence in this section, and that in the final verse (10:16), of the key root *mlk*, whence are derived the Hebrew words for 'rule', 'king', and 'kingdom'. Instead of *melek* ('king') we have the much-debated term *nāgîd* (RSV 'prince') in 9:16 and 10:1, while the peculiar use of the verb *'āṣar*, somewhat generously rendered by 'rule' in various modern versions of 9:17, excludes the obvious candidate *mālak* ('to rule, reign'). The indications are that Samuel is anointing Saul to a circumscribed

exercise of 'kingship' that does not usurp his own unique prophetic
authority.

1 Samuel 10:17-27

The next tableau is a short account of an assembly at Mizpah, at
which the divine approval of Saul's candidature was expressed
publicly in the disposition of the sacred lot. ('The lot is cast into the
lap, but the decision is wholly from the LORD' [Prov. 16:33].) First of
all, the section's ambivalent attitude towards the monarchy—despite
the divine approval—deserves special comment. On the one hand we
have verses 17-19 reasserting the critical tone of ch. 8, on the other
verses 24-27 with their unstinted enthusiasm for Saul's appointment.
To regard 10:17-27—or even 10:17-25a—as a narrative continuation
of an anti-monarchical source which began with ch. 8 is, therefore, to
over-simplify the situation.

A complication of a different sort is introduced at verse 21,
according to which the lot falls on someone who has actually
absented himself from the proceedings. Our ignorance of the workings
of the sacred lot may account for the problem; nevertheless, a few
scholars have concluded that there is an anomaly and that it has
arisen from an inexact suturing of two different traditions about
Saul's election, the one associating it with the sacred lot and the
other with his physical stature. Whether we agree with this or not,
there is no denying that great stress is laid upon Saul's physical
appearance, as if this in itself was confirmation of his kingly vocation.
And, to some extent, this is how it may have seemed to the popular
mind, for, as a mythological text from Ugarit testifies, the near-
eastern king could fail to measure up to his task—literally! Poor
Athtar, who aspired to Baal's throne in the epic 'Baal and Mot', was
judged unworthy because his legs were too short to reach the
footstool and his head did not reach the top! But with Saul the limits
of this view of kingliness are exposed, being expressly repudiated in
the story of the anointing of his successor: 'man looks on the outward
appearance, but the LORD looks on the heart' (1 Sam. 16:7). It is
paradoxical, then, that in this section in which Saul is proclaimed as
God's choice, by the device of the lot, the criterion of physical
endowment, rich in popular appeal, is thrust into the centre. So,
while 'your king whom you [the people] have chosen' (8:18) has
become 'the man whom *the LORD* has chosen' (10:24), there may be a

hint here that from the outset Saul's hold on kingship is less than secure. And once we have begun to think along these lines, it is even possible to interpret the whole episode of the lot-casting, which on the surface seems to be such a positive affirmation of Saul's divine election as king, as an expression of Yahweh's displeasure at the new development; the two comparable episodes in the Old Testament (Jos. 7:16-26; 1 Sam. 14:38-46) concern the uncovering of someone believed to have brought harm upon the community.

The subjection of the new institution of monarchy to prophetic authority, implicit in all that happens at Mizpah, is ratified in Samuel's memorandum defining 'the rights and duties of the kingship' (Heb. *mišpaṭ hammᵉlūkāh*, 10:25). Despite the formal similarity of this expression to 'the ways of the king' (Heb. *mišpaṭ hammelek*) in 8:9, 11, a clear distinction between the two should be made; it is the difference between prescription and description, no less. Again, the kingly law-book of Deuteronomy 17:18-20 reflects the same concern that kings should rule according to divine law, yet any closer relationship between the two 'books' can be established only at the cost of disregarding obvious points of difference between them.

1 Samuel 11:1-15

Saul's first opportunity to display his mettle came about a month after the Mizpah convocation—if we follow the (probably) superior text of 10:27b–11:1 found in a Qumran fragment and reflected in the Septuagint (cf. NEB)—when the Transjordanian town of Jabesh-gilead came under siege from the Ammonite king Nahash and his army. The absence in Israel of a central government, as also of a unified military command, during this period was doubtless a factor in the Jabesh-gileadites' initial offer to become vassals of Nahash. They were isolated from the bulk of the Israelite community, and not hopeful of effective brotherly assistance from the other side of the Jordan. But Nahash's terms were inhumane, and they were driven to issue the appeal which brought Saul to the rescue.

Of the several pericopes making up 1 Samuel 8-12, this one is usually held to represent most closely the circumstances in which Saul became king. It is a straightforward narrative of deliverance in which the crisis produces the hero much as in the stories of deliverance in the book of Judges; the way in which Saul, on hearing of the predicament of Jabesh-gilead, is seized by the divine Spirit

(v. 6) has parallels in the accounts of Othniel, Gideon, and Jephthah, whose timely inspiration brought victory in battle. Whether ch. 11 by itself suggests that Saul, until this point, had been a private citizen is a matter of debate. In verses 4f. it is not obvious that the Jabesh-gileadite emissaries came specifically looking for Saul, yet, on the other hand, it is questionable whether the 'bucolic butcher' (so Halpern) of verse 7 would have acted as he did if he was previously unknown among the tribes. With regard to this latter point, there is the complication that the reference to Samuel is frequently treated as a secondary addition, on the ground that Samuel was old (cf. 8:1, but see 15:33!) and unlikely to figure in a call to arms. But presumably Samuel's name here represents authority rather than derring-do.

One question that has not been sufficiently aired is whether the narrative is deliberately structured to maximize the comparison between Saul and the deliverers of yesteryear, as a way of saying that, even when Israel has a king, deliverance may still come in the old way. That could then be a statement about ideal kingship, insofar as an ideal may be contained within a compromise, and might even carry the implication that the old pre-monarchical order was sufficient for Israel's crises, rather as we found in the account of 'Samuel's victory' in ch. 7. We should not, therefore, limit ourselves to the mere observation that Saul is a 'transitional' figure, as between judgeship and monarchy, in 11:1-15. That he undoubtedly is, but the text may have subtler points for our consideration.

The sequel to the relief of Jabesh-gilead was that Saul was offered the crown and a permanent contract by his grateful fellow-Israelites. Thus, even if the reference to the *renewal* of the kingdom in verse 14 is taken as a secondary harmonization with the Mizpah narrative preceding, both the biblical account and the theoretical reconstruction are agreed that monarchy came to Israel by the will of the people.

1 Samuel 12:1-25

M. Noth, as we saw in Chapter 1, highlighted this section as Deuteronomistic oration marking the end of the era of the Judges. It consists almost entirely of utterances by Samuel to 'all Israel' (v. 1), in which he first denounces them for their headlong plunge into monarchy in spite of their creditable salvation-history to date, and then extends to them the possibility of safe conduct in the future, provided that they remain loyal to Yahweh. This is uncompromising 'two-way theology', and it ends with a warning of catastrophe that reads like an epitaph on the kingdom of Judah: 'But if you still do wickedly, you shall be swept away, both you and your king' (v. 25). McCarter, as a matter of interest, sees this verse as the sole exilic intervention by the Deuteronomistic circle in 1 Samuel.

Ch. 12 is a companion-piece to 8:1-22. However, not only is the earlier condemnation now repeated, but the grounds on which the popular demand for a king had been made are decisively rejected. There the unfitness of Samuel's sons to succeed him in his role as judge had been meant to silence the prophet's protest; here Samuel ensures that 'the old order' is judged on his own record, not that of his sons. (That record seems deliberately to have been summarized so as to contrast with the sketch of kingly rapacity in 8:11-18.) The people had pointed to the military advantages; Samuel recalls the 'righteous acts of the LORD' (v. 7), which account for both set-back and success, from the Exodus to the siege of Jabesh-gilead. However, the Samuel speeches in this chapter represent an advance on expostulation. The reality of the monarchy is accepted and a *modus vivendi* is outlined. Provided that there is no more rebelling against Yahweh, the new institution can be integrated into the already-existing covenantal relationship between Yahweh and Israel. While the word 'covenant' does not appear in the chapter, there is sufficient covenant terminology (cf. McCarthy) to justify this reading of Samuel's closing admonitions. Under the new constitution there must also be a diminished role for Samuel, the reformulation of whose duties—more moral than contractual—in terms of prayer and teaching states something akin to the later prophetic norm.

Conclusion

The social and religious implications of the replacement of the old tribal system in Israel by a central, typically near-eastern monarchy were fully appreciated by the compiler of 1 Samuel 7-12. And what is true of the whole is true of each of the parts: Samuel, somewhat analogously to Moses in the Pentateuchal traditions, is ever-present, presiding over the constitutional démarche while at the same time deeply critical of it. Of his involvement in the events leading up to Saul's enthronement we need scarcely be in doubt. Samuel, we may judge, serves also as the mouthpiece of the compiler of these chapters. The compiler apparently did not think very highly of the monarchy, notwithstanding the assurances of various scholars that chs 8 and 12 are miscalled when they are pronounced 'anti-monarchical'. (How this can be so when the text repeatedly states that the introduction of the monarchy was not the will of Yahweh, and was conceded only under protest, has still to be explained.) For the accounts reflect much more than 'the vacillation which must inevitably accompany so radical a departure from custom', to quote one such critic; nor does the contextualization of the original demand in the malpractices of Samuel's sons (8:1-3) have any significant softening effect.

Leaving aside the *sotto voce* contribution of ch. 7, we note that the chapters on monarchy begin and end with strident denunciation (chs 8 and 12). B.S. Childs, in pursuit of his 'canonical perspective', takes this a step further with his observation that, if the compiler's arrangement of his material is classified according as it is 'for' or 'against', a purposeful symmetry emerges. If, says Childs, the 'pro-monarchical' narratives are represented by 'A' and the 'anti-monarchical' by 'B', the resultant schema is B-A-B-A-B, with the 'anti-monarchical' material constituting both centre and circumference. How appropriate such a characterization of the several sections is may be judged from the foregoing discussion, not least in relation to the central episode at Mizpah. Nevertheless, as an appraisal of the overall 'message' of these chapters it can hardly be faulted.

Further Reading

Studies of a general nature:

D.J. McCarthy, 'The Inauguration of Monarchy in Israel: A Form-Critical Study of 1 Samuel 8-12', *Interpretation* 27 (1973), 401-412.

B.C. Birch, *The Rise of the Israelite Monarchy: The Growth and Development of 1 Samuel 7-15* (SBL Dissertation Series, 27), Missoula: Scholars Press, 1976.

T.N.D. Mettinger, *King and Messiah. The Civil and Sacral Legitimation of the Israelite Kings* (Coniectanea Biblica, Old Testament Series, 8), Lund: C.W.K. Gleerup, 1976, 80-98.

T. Ishida, *The Royal Dynasties in Israel. A Study on the Formation and Development of Royal-Dynastic Ideology* (BZAW, 142), Berlin/New York: Walter de Gruyter, 1977, 26-41.

A.D.H. Mayes, 'The Rise of the Israelite Monarchy', *ZAW* 90 (1978), 1-19.

Mayes, in Hayes—Miller, 293-297.

M. Tsevat, 'The Biblical Account of the Foundation of the Monarchy in Israel', in *The Meaning of the Book of Job and Other Biblical Studies: Essays on the Literature and Religion of the Hebrew Bible*, New York: Ktav, 1980, 77-99.

B. Halpern, *The Constitution of the Monarchy in Israel* (Harvard Semitic Monographs, 25), Chico: Scholars Press, 1981, 149-174.

Childs, 277f.

Significant contributions in German include:

A. Weiser, *Samuel. Seine geschichtliche Aufgabe und religiöse Bedeutung. Traditionsgeschichtliche Untersuchungen zu 1. Samuel 7-12* (FRLANT, 81), Göttingen: Vandenhoeck & Ruprecht, 1962.

H.J. Boecker, *Die Beurteilung der Anfänge des Königtums in den deuteronomistischen Abschnitten des 1. Samuelbuches. Ein Beitrag zum Problem des 'deuteronomistischen Geschichtswerks'* (WMANT, 31), Neukirchen-Vluyn: Neukirchener Verlag, 1969.

T. Veijola, *Das Königtum in der Beurteilung der deuteronomistischen Historiographie: eine redaktionsgeschichtliche Untersuchung*, Helsinki: Suomalainen Tiedeakatemia, 1977.

F. Crüsemann, *Der Widerstand gegen das Königtum. Die antiköniglichen Texte des Alten Testamentes und der Kampf um den frühen israelitischen Staat* (WMANT, 49), Neukirchen-Vluyn: Neukirchener Verlag, 1978.

Studies of individual sections:

I. Mendelsohn, 'Samuel's Denunciation of Kingship in the Light of the Akkadian Documents from Ugarit', *BASOR* 143 (1956), 17-22 (see also the comments on Mendelsohn by A.F. Rainey in L.R. Fisher [ed.], *Ras Shamra Parallels*, II [Analecta Orientalia, 50], Rome: Pontificium Institutum Biblicum, 1975, 93-98).

B.C. Birch, 'The Development of the Tradition on the Anointing of Saul in 1 Sam 9:1-10:16', *JBL* 90 (1971), 55-68.

Birch, 'The Choosing of Saul at Mizpah', *CBQ* 37 (1975), 447-457.

R.E. Clements, 'The Deuteronomistic Interpretation of the Founding of the Monarchy in I Sam. VIII', *VT* 24 (1974), 398-410.

J.R. Vannoy, *Covenant Renewal at Gilgal: A Study of I Samuel 11:14–12:25*, Cherry Hill: Mack Publishing Company, 1978 (includes a chapter on the literary criticism of 1 Samuel 8-12).

Z. Ben-Barak, 'The Mizpah Covenant (I Sam 10 25)—The Source of the Israelite Monarchic Covenant', *ZAW* 91 (1979), 30-43.

For discussion of the key term *nāgîd* see:

Mettinger, 64-79, 151-184.

Halpern, 1-11.

5

THE REIGN
OF SAUL

WHILE IT IS true that the whole of 1 Samuel 13-31 is concerned with events during the reign of Saul, it appears that the narrator or compiler responsible for the present contours of the narrative wished to suggest that the account of the reign is effectively confined to chs 13-15. The beginning is clearly marked with an accession formula (13:1)—ironically incomplete, as if to signal the outcome of Saul's reign!—of the kind frequently used in the books of Kings (e.g. 2 Kgs 14:1f.; 15:1f.). The question of the ending is not quite so straightforward, but is potentially more interesting. First we must note that ch. 14 already presents what might be called a 'concluding summary' of Saul's reign (vv. 47-52). But we should be ill-advised to seek here the evidence of the negative editing to which we have referred, for these verses show a high regard for Saul as king and military leader. The summary may have been put here simply because the defeat of the Philistines was seen as the high point in the story of the house of Saul.

In the concluding verses of ch. 15, on the other hand, there are elements which seem deliberately to suggest that Saul's virtual decease takes place at this point. First there is the instant parable that Samuel makes of his torn robe, when he tells Saul that the kingdom of Israel has been torn from him 'this day' (v. 28). This announcement is noticeably more personal and immediate than its predecessor in 13:13f., where Saul's rejection is subsumed under the rejection of his house. Then we are informed that Samuel never again saw Saul (v. 35), which as a statement of fact is challenged by 1 Samuel 19:24, but is apparently the narrator's way of emphasizing the irreconcilability of prophet and king. Saul, cast aside by the prophet of Yahweh, can no longer claim to rule under divine auspices: his reign is as good as finished. This point is reinforced in the statement that Samuel 'mourned' (RSV 'grieved') for Saul, since the verb in question (*'ābal*) normally occurs in connection with mourning for the dead. (The reference to the execution of Agag, king of the Amalekites, in vv. 32f. is therefore peculiarly appropriate to the context.)

It is entirely in keeping with this presentation of God's rejection of Saul, then, that there should immediately follow, in ch. 16, the story of the anointing of the next king of Israel. The king is dead! Long live the king! Chs 16-31 are indeed set in the reign of Saul, but it is a sound instinct on the part of a number of scholars that has credited these chapters to 'The History of David's Rise', for, whether or not we detect an independent account behind this History (see Chapter 6), there can be no doubt as to its orientation towards the rising star of David. Officially, and certainly from Saul's point of view, the David of the History is in rebellion against his king, but, as has been well observed, the real rebel in the story is Saul, who will go to almost any length in order to thwart the divine purpose.

In chs 13-14 there are, nevertheless, enough indications of sympathy with Saul to suggest that they bring us near to 'historic reality'. In this connection, the tone of the reference to Saul's defeat of the Amalekites in 14:48 is interesting in view of the deprecatory account of the Amalekite campaign in the next chapter. In fact, both the archival summary in 14:47f. and the theologically-filtered narratives in chs 13-15 bear witness to Saul's attempts to free Israelite tribal territory from the menace of encroaching neighbours. A sympathetic reading of 1 Samuel 13-31 might even credit Saul with having a 'strategy', according to which he established his hold on the centre and south of the country, prior to his final and unsuccessful venture against the Philistines in the north (cf. Hauer). However, the main problem raised by chs 13-15 is not that of assessing Saul's military achievements, but of establishing the precise grounds on which he was judged unworthy to occupy the throne of Israel.

There are two separate pronouncements on the matter, and, though both are linked with Gilgal, they relate to distinct sets of circumstances: to Saul's precipitate offering of sacrifice before battle in ch. 13, and to his failure to prosecute the 'ban' with the required vigour in ch. 15. Common to both narratives, and in particular to the respective charges that are laid against Saul, is his failure to comply fully with Samuel's instruction. Already in 10:8, at the end of Samuel's private commissioning of Saul, an apparently detached logion—which may have stood in a closer relationship to 13:7b-15a at an earlier stage—establishes that Saul's exercise of kingship must satisfy the test of obedience: Saul has to wait at Gilgal until Samuel arrives ('until I come to you'). This is the background to the prophet's excoriation of Saul in 13:13f. Saul in a rapidly deteriorating situation had taken it upon himself to offer the burnt offering, and immediately Samuel, as if monitoring the king's behaviour off-stage, stepped forward to remonstrate with him. It is a straightforward question of obedience, and Saul has failed. The command of 10:8 therefore stands like a tree of knowledge in Saul's Eden, and contingent upon his obedience is the possibility expressed in 13:13: 'for now the LORD would have established your kingdom over Israel for ever'. Other explanations of Saul's offence, such as that by offering sacrifice he, a layman, intruded into the sacral realm, or that his precipitateness betrayed a lack of trust in God, are probably unnecessary. Cultic infringement by a king, moreover, seems to be unlikely as the substance of a charge in view of other references in Samuel—Kings where David and Solomon, for example, are said to have offered sacrifice (2 Sam. 6:17f.; 24:25; 1 Kgs 3:3f.).

Irrespective of the favourable glimpses of Saul in ch. 14, and of the possibility of an underlying source sympathetic towards him, the general effect of this chapter, even without the help of a denunciation by Samuel, is to show him falling far short of the standard expected of one who was appointed to save Israel from the hand of the Philistines (cf. 9:16). In fact, it is Jonathan who achieves the success against the Philistines in this chapter—just as he is credited with the defeat of the Philistine garrison at Geba (13:3)—while Saul's contribution is, by his recklessness, to limit the scale of the success and to leave the life of his hero-son dangling by a thread. Here, as elsewhere in 1 Samuel, the contrast between the behaviour of Saul and Jonathan is pronounced. Whereas Saul's offence in ch. 13 is closely linked with the rapid depletion of his forces (vv. 8, 11), it is Jonathan who, alone with his armour-bearer, speaks the word of faith in ch. 14: 'nothing can hinder the LORD from saving by many or by few' (v. 6). Jonathan, moreover, receives divine confirmation of the rightness of his stratagem (vv. 8-12), even without the oracular aid available to his father; and the happy conclusion of his exploit was that 'the LORD delivered Israel that day' (v. 23). But the second half of the chapter casts a different light on the day's events by describing the triplex consequences of Saul's imposition of a fast upon his warriors 'until . . . I am avenged on my enemies' (v. 24). To this overheated pronouncement can be attributed a curtailment of the Israelites' mopping-up operation, an infringement of ritual law, and the jeopardizing of Jonathan's life.

With reference to the first of these inconveniences Jonathan declares that his father 'has troubled (*'ākar*) the land' (v. 29), using the keynote verb in the story of Achan, who 'troubled' Israel (cf. Josh. 7:25) by his disregard of the 'ban' imposed by Joshua at the siege of Jericho (cf. Josh. 6:17ff.). In view of the other parallels between the two narratives, and in particular the identifying of the guilty party by lot, it is interesting to read Jonathan's use of *'ākar* in the light of Joshua 7. The parallel in the first instance must be between Achan and *Jonathan*, for the latter, by his breach of the interdict, stands to 'trouble' Israel, as is evident from verse 37. Jonathan, however, makes a pre-emptive strike in verse 29, by stating that *his father* has 'troubled' the land by his imposition of the oath. (We might compare the later disagreement between Ahab and Elijah as to which of them was 'troubling' Israel [1 Kgs 18:17f.].) The correspondence with Joshua 7 therefore encourages us to think of ch. 14 as generically a 'troubling-narrative', but with the quite subtle twist that the key term is applied, not to the technically guilty Jonathan, but to Saul.

Verses 31-35 deal with the second unfortunate consequence of Saul's intervention, though in such a way as to recover a little of his reputation for him as he is shown acting decisively in defence of ritual law. The notice concerning the raising of the first altar (v. 35) may also be laudatory in its intention. But, whereas in this brief episode Saul acts like a leader of his people, the next shows him having to bow to their superior good sense when Jonathan's peccadillo is disclosed and Saul would have him pay the full penalty (v. 45). Despite his previous disloyal remark (v. 29) and Saul's willingness to let him die, there is no suggestion that either Saul or his priest manipulated the lot as a means of getting rid of Jonathan. Verse 39 reverberates with irony, not conspiracy. The real point of the narrative is that Saul, having by his rashness brought things to such a pass and not even now recoiling from the dreadful consequences, is prevented from acting by his incredulous warriors, who find no difficulty in drawing out the proper implications of the day's success. The last word is with them: 'he [Jonathan] has wrought with God this day' (v.45).

Even ch. 14, then, despite its occasionally more positive tendencies, constitutes a powerful criticism of Saul's exercise of kingship, partly by highlighting the success of Jonathan, and partly by its depiction of Saul lurching from one complication to the next. When a list of Saul's successes 'against his enemies on every side' (v. 47) is appended to what is essentially a story about Jonathan's prowess and Saul's weakness, the reader may even be forgiven for reading the one in the light of the other.

With ch. 15 obedience becomes even more of an issue than in ch. 13, as is most superficially evident in the five occurrences of the verb 'obey' in verses 19-24. Since there is some dispute as to how successfully the chapter presses the charge of disobedience against Saul, it is important to observe the specificity of the instructions given in verse 3: there is no possibility of misunderstanding. Nor does the narrator suggest that there was any misunderstanding, inasmuch as he notes in verse 9 that Saul and his men 'spared' Agag and the best of the spoil, in direct contravention, it is implied, of the original command. Neither does he show any sympathy for Saul's claim that the exception was made in order to provide for a victory celebration 'before the LORD' (v. 15). Furthermore, the force of the statement that the people 'were not willing' (*lō' 'ābû*) to destroy everything (v. 9) should not be missed. This is a quite strong expression, and, in view of its association with the Hebrew root *mrh* ('rebel') in several Old Testament passages (e.g. Dt. 1:26; Is. 30:9; Ezek. 3:7ff.; 20:8), it is not too far-fetched to link its occurrence here with Samuel's reference to 'rebellion' in verse 23. (We may note Brown-Driver-Briggs' listing of a class of references where this verb [*'ābāh*], with negative, is used 'especially of perverse Israel' [*A Hebrew and English Lexicon*, 2].) Therefore, let Saul pretext what he will, it will be a poor postscript to God's previously-announced verdict: 'he has turned back from following me, and has not performed my commandments' (v. 11).

So it is plain that, in the narrator's eyes, Saul is guilty of wilful disobedience. Pleas of mitigation, as that Saul actually did obey Samuel's instructions to the best of his ability, and that his short-fall was attributable to a different understanding of the requirements of the 'ban'—would the sacrifice at Gilgal not have qualified as a partial observance of the 'ban'?—may be entered on his behalf by the modern reader, but not on the basis of the biblical text. Not even Saul's presence at Gilgal can be taken as an earnest of his intention to

complete the requirements of the 'ban', since, questions of prevarica-
tion apart, he could have offered his sacrifices and then shared the
rest of the spoil around. Samuel, in a telling phrase coloured by its
previous occurrence in 14:32, says as much when he accuses him of
'swooping on the spoil' (v. 19). But perhaps the most paradoxical
feature of all, when chs 14 and 15 are read together, is that the man
who was prepared to see his own son die because of his rash
imposition of an oath was willing to spare Agag the king of the
Amalekites.

A final question remains to be asked: Are we to understand that
Saul was doomed from the start? D.M. Gunn answers affirmatively
and supports his position with some useful points. He detects, in the
first place, a deliberate contrast between God's instruction to Samuel
to 'appoint for *them* [the people] a king' (1 Sam. 8:22) and his later
announcement that he had provided *for himself* a king from the sons
of Jesse (1 Sam. 16:1). On this reading, Saul is a king who cannot
succeed because he was never truly acknowledged by God as his
choice. And, according to Gunn, the reappearance of the rejection-
motif in 15:23, 26, reinforcing 13:13f., has a similar significance, in
that the rejection of Saul is now seen as God's planned response to
the people's earlier rejection of himself (cf. 8:7; 10:19). Thus would
Gunn deal with the problem of the austerity of God and of Samuel
his representative, and of the seeming triviality of the offences which
resulted in Saul's downfall. For why should Saul be deprived of his
throne when David did worse and prospered? But if Saul was indeed
a king 'given in anger' (cf. Hos. 13:11), then we may begin to
understand why he was allowed such a comparatively small margin
of error. These are valuable insights, and yet the biblical text has
other elements which discourage us from proceeding too far in that
direction. We have already referred to 13:13b, noteworthy for its
implications in the present context. It is significant, too, that both
rejection sayings in 15:23, 26 insist that Yahweh's repudiation of
Saul came in response to Saul's own repudiation of Yahweh.

Further Reading

Studies dealing with literary and psychological aspects of the Saul tradition:

W.L. Humphreys, 'The Tragedy of King Saul: A Study of the
Structure of 1 Samuel 9-31', *JSOT* 6 (1978), 18-27.

Humphreys, 'The Rise and Fall of King Saul: A Study of an Ancient Narrative Stratum in 1 Samuel', *JSOT* 18 (1980), 74-90.

Humphreys, 'From Tragic Hero to Villain: a Study of the Figure of Saul and the Development of 1 Samuel', *JSOT* 22 (1982), 95-117.

D.M. Gunn, *The Fate of King Saul. An Interpretation of a Biblical Story* (*JSOT* Suppl., 14), Sheffield: JSOT Press, 1980.

Gunn, 'A Man Given over to Trouble: The Story of King Saul', in *Images of Man and God: Old Testament Short Stories in Literary Focus* (ed. B.O. Long; Bible and Literature Series, 1), Sheffield: Almond Press, 1981, 89-112.

E.M. Good, 'Saul: The Tragedy of Greatness', in *Irony in the Old Testament*, 2nd edn (Bible and Literature Series, 3), Sheffield: Almond Press, 1981, 56-80.

Historical and administrative aspects of Saul's reign are discussed by:

C.E. Hauer, 'The Shape of Saulide Strategy', *CBQ* 31 (1969), 153-167.

J. Blenkinsopp, 'The Quest of the Historical Saul', in *No Famine in the Land. Studies in Honor of J.L. McKenzie* (ed. J.W. Flanagan, A.W. Robinson), Missoula: Scholars Press (for The Institute for Antiquity and Christianity, Claremont), 1975, 75-99.

K.W. Whitelam, *The Just King. Monarchical Judicial Authority in Ancient Israel* (*JSOT* Suppl., 12), Sheffield: JSOT Press, 1979, 71-89.

A.D.H. Mayes, in Hayes—Miller, 322-331.

The following articles deal with individual sections (principally ch. 14):

J. Blenkinsopp, 'Jonathan's Sacrilege. 1 SM 14, 1-46', *CBQ* 26 (1964), 423-449.

J.M. Miller, 'Saul's Rise to Power: Some Observations Concerning 1 Sam 9:1–10:16; 10:26–11:15 and 13:2–14:46', *CBQ* 36 (1974), 157-174.

D. Jobling, 'Saul's Fall and Jonathan's Rise: Tradition and Redaction in 1 Sam 14:1-46', *JBL* 95 (1976), 367-376.

Other studies of importance include:

D. Jobling, 'Jonathan: A Structural Study in 1 Samuel', in *The Sense of Biblical Narrative: Three Structural Analyses in the Old Testament* (*JSOT* Suppl., 7), Sheffield: JSOT Press, 1978, 4-25.

H. Seebass, *David, Saul und das Wesen des biblischen Glaubens*, Neukirchen-Vluyn: Neukirchener Verlag, 1980 (a fair proportion of this book is devoted to literary-critical issues in 1 Sam. 7-15).

6

THE STORY
OF DAVID

THE BULK OF 1 and 2 Samuel (1 Sam. 16–2 Sam. 24) centres on the career of David of Bethlehem who, after many alarums and excursions, succeeded Saul on the throne of Israel. Saul himself does not disappear from view until 1 Samuel 31, which recounts how he met an inglorious death on the hills of Gilboa following a disastrous encounter with the Philistines, yet even while the biographies of the two are intertwined it is the interests of David that are capital.

Thanks in no small way to Rost's 1926 study, it has become fashionable to divide the story of David into two main units which are thought to represent two originally independent narratives. The 'History of David's Rise', a kind of *Bildungsroman* (narrative tracing the development of a character), follows David's early career to the point where he has been acknowledged as king by all the tribes of Israel and has taken up residence in Jerusalem, his newly-acquired capital (2 Sam. 5). The reign of David in Jerusalem, and particularly the internal problems of the royal house in this period, is the subject of the 'Succession Narrative' which occupies most of the remainder of 2 Samuel and extends as far as 1 Kings 2. This will serve as a convenient division of the material, even if the remanent magnetism of Rost's work is now not so strong as it used to be.

THE HISTORY OF DAVID'S RISE

1. **Delimitation**

The idea of an independent account of David's progress towards the throne was not original to Rost—it is anticipated in, for example, Julius Wellhausen's *Prolegomena to the History of Israel* (first published in English in 1885)—but it was his brief discussion that did most to give it respectability. Even so, it was fully thirty years before the subject was again seriously investigated, first in two or three dissertations and then in a number of articles in journals. The first published monograph to deal with the 'History of David's Rise' was by J.H. Grønbaek, in 1971.

Rost's version of the History was, we might note, but a shadow of what was to come, for it comprised only pieces and fragments from 1 Samuel 23:1 through to 2 Samuel 5:10. In the subsequent discussions, on the other hand, the tendency has been to regard it as a more comprehensive entity and to find its starting-point considerably earlier than Rost had suggested. Thus, whereas Ward begins at 1 Samuel 16:14, Weiser favours verse 1 of the same chapter, while Grønbaek, followed by Mettinger, goes back to 15:1.

Weiser's inclusion of 16:1-13 is in part necessitated by his extension of the far boundary of the History to include 2 Samuel 7—which indeed he designates the 'keystone' of the narrative—for 2 Samuel 7:8 ('I took you from the pasture') presupposes 16:1-13. Mettinger, for whom David is 'the secret Messiah' in the History of David's Rise, maintains that, if the narrative is meant to glorify David, then we might expect its several references to Saul as 'the LORD's anointed' (e.g. 1 Sam. 24:6; 26:9) to be counterbalanced by a report of the secret anointing of David such as we have in 16:1-13. Against this, Crüsemann notes that the anointing of David by Samuel is not mentioned again, whereas David himself repeatedly refers to Saul as 'the LORD's anointed' in the History of David's Rise. Grønbaek argues that his more radical suggestion of 15:1 as the starting-point of the History is supported by the presence of a summary of Saul's reign at the end of ch. 14, and by the reference to David in 15:28, this latter because it looks forward to his anointing and should not be divorced from it.

We have already noted that Weiser's version extended beyond the traditional boundary of 2 Samuel 5:10 to include ch. 7, and in this he has the support of Mettinger. Mettinger points out that David's victories over the Philistines, as recounted in 5:17-25, mark the fulfilment of the promise mentioned in 3:18. Moreover, in the prominence given to oracular consultation in 5:17-25 he detects a characteristic feature of the History. And because of a number of verbal linkages between 2 Samuel 5:17-25 and 6:1-23 he concludes that these two sections were transmitted together, both being integral to the History. Again, Mettinger argues that the allusion to David's future kingship in 3:9f. points forward to, and presupposes, the Nathan oracle—as also does 5:2, which he regards as dependent upon 7:7f. Mettinger is therefore of the opinion that the History concluded with some form of the Nathan oracle (which oracle, indeed, he regards as being possibly the joint property of the History of David's Rise and the Succession Narrative). It is to be observed too, in this connection, that Abigail's speech in 1 Samuel 25, and especially the assurance that David will have a 'sure house' (v. 28), clearly articulates the ideology of the Nathan oracle. Furthermore, if 2 Samuel 6 is apportioned to the History of David's Rise—and we have witnessed its eviction from the Ark Narrative (see Chapter 3)!— it will tend, by reason of the relatedness of the subject-matter, to draw ch. 7 with it (cf. the linking of the themes of ark and dynasty in Ps. 132). Again, as in the case of the Ark Narrative, we have to note that not all those who have discussed the subject of the History of David's Rise are convinced that it ever existed as an independent literary entity.

2. Theme

'What thou wouldst highly, that wouldst thou holily'
(*Macbeth*, I, 5)

From the uncertainties of source delimitation we turn to the question of theme, where we are assured of more palpable gains. Whatever our preferred picture of David, and however we may adjudge his motives, the attitude of the narrator toward his subject in these chapters is utterly transparent, and fittingly epitomized in Lady Macbeth's unjustified, as it happened, appraisal of her husband. At the same time, the sinuous account of David's progress towards the throne discloses more than a peccadillo, for there is no lack of candour; the David of the History of David's Rise is 'a mixture of gipsy and Franciscan', to borrow the composer Ferenc (Franz) Liszt's description of himself. Nevertheless, it is insisted that in one vital respect David conducted himself impeccably on his way to the throne. Anointed under prophetic auspices though he himself had been, he steadfastly declined to prise the kingdom from Saul by harming 'the LORD's anointed', even when the eschewal of violence prolonged the threat to his own life. In two complementary scenes in 1 Samuel 24 and 26 the issue is sharpened dramatically, when David twice has

Saul at his mercy and is incited by others to seize a 'God-given' chance of revenge. But, as we shall see, he did not succumb to the temptation to lay violent hands on Saul.

Essentially the same point is made in connection with David's reactions to the news of the deaths of Saul, Abner, and Eshbaal. At the time of Saul's death David was technically a vassal of the Philistines, but it is made clear that in no way was he responsible for what took place at Gilboa; indeed, he was dismissed from the Philistine attack force because of a suspicion that he would suddenly turn on his masters in the heat of the battle (1 Sam. 29:1-11). Later, when the Amalekite escapee spun his self-regarding account of Saul's last minutes, David interpreted his glosses differently, and the man forfeited his life for lifting his hand against the anointed king of Israel (2 Sam. 1:1-16). And as assuredly as the question *cui bono?* (Who benefits?) was asked when Abner and Eshbaal fell victims to separate acts of treachery, the respective accounts insist on David's non-complicity, dwelling at length on his horrified reactions when the news reached him (2 Sam. 3:28-39; 4:9-12).

The rationale behind this presentation of David in the History of David's Rise is encapsulated in Abigail's speech in 1 Samuel 25, in a sentence which stresses the long-term advantages of a clear conscience over any momentary gain from self-indulgence: 'And when the LORD has done to my lord according to all the good that he has spoken concerning you, and has appointed you prince over Israel, my lord shall have no cause of grief, or pangs of conscience, for having shed blood without cause or for my lord taking vengeance himself' (vv. 30f.). We may even go so far as to say that 1 Samuel 25 describes a critical episode in the account of relations between David and Saul, and this despite the fact that Saul is not mentioned in forty-two verses of narrative. For the story of Nabal stands catalytically between the two accounts of David's sparing of Saul noted above. These two are usually regarded as variant accounts of the same incident, by virtue of their common theme and shared features, and despite notable differences of various sorts. But whether separate incidents or sibling accounts with independent oral pre-histories, they have distinct functions to fulfil in the unfolding of David's attitude to Saul, as becomes very evident when ch. 25 is brought into the discussion.

In the first account David does not actually harm Saul, though he humiliates him and performs what has every appearance of being a symbolic gesture of rebellion against his master (24:4). Smitten with compunction for even the limited outrage that he had committed, David berates his men for inciting him to outright violence, and ensures that Saul leaves the cave unmolested (24:6f.). The issue is reintroduced in ch. 26, but with significant variations, and most particularly in the way David responds to Abishai's offer to eliminate Saul at a stroke. Once more vengeful impetuosity had pleaded theological justification, for 'God has given your enemy into your hand this day' (26:8; cf. 24:4), but this time there was no symbolic act, nor so much as a hint of weakness on David's part. There is expressed, however, a truth complementary to that of Saul's sacro-sanctity as 'the LORD's anointed', viz. that Saul will receive his due reward from God to whom he is accountable: 'As the LORD lives, the LORD will smite him; or his day shall come to die; or he shall go down into battle and perish' (26:10). This is a markedly more assured David than the one who had crouched in the cave by Engedi, and the grounds of his assurance are to be found in the bridging chapter in which, to judge from a number of verbal echoes of earlier chapters dealing with Saul, Nabal stands proxy for Saul.

Even more pointed than any of these cross-references, however, is that statement in 26:10, 'the LORD will smite him', for it directly recalls 25:38, 'And about ten days later *the LORD smote Nabal*; and he died'. Because socially and psychologically Nabal so nearly approximates to Saul, his death, consequent upon his refusal to help David and his band, becomes a 'type' foreshadowing the death of Saul himself. With this assurance David may retain clean hands and yet achieve his goal!

A decidedly less favourable estimation of the David of the History of David's Rise is given by Tomoo Ishida (VanderKam writes in similar vein) who sees him as an opportunist rebel waging a vigorous guerrilla war against Saul, and so compelling him to make repeated efforts to flush him out of the Judaean wilderness (cf. 1 Sam. 23:15, 25f.; 24:1f.; 26:2). Further evidence of David's usurpatory intent is found in his association with a band of several hundred malcontents (cf. 1 Sam. 22:1f.), in what Ishida calls 'David's ambush' on the basis of 1 Samuel 22:8, 13, and in David's willingness to fight on the Philistine side at Gilboa. Then, says Ishida, we have to explain why David was in military contention with Saul's son and successor Eshbaal, if he was indeed the irenic heir-in-waiting of the History of David's Rise. In reality, according to Ishida, Saul was a popular king—a fact not to be obscured by misinterpretation of 1 Samuel 22:8, which is merely the utterance of a mistrustful individual given to overstatement. So jealousy alone, claims Ishida, fails to explain Saul's intense hatred of David; it was the latter's plotting which drove the two so far apart. And, finally, the narrator's 'vehement advocacy of David's innocence' in the History is interpreted by Ishida as evidence to the contrary. Detailed refutation of these points would be tedious in a study of this sort, and would court the danger of propounding an equally one-sided view of David's behaviour; nevertheless, a few comments can be briefly made.

In the first place, there is no indication in the narrative, whether by overt statement or indirect hint, that David ever sought to deploy his freebooters against Saul. Aggression on David's part was not lacking, as the Nabal episode well shows (cf. 1 Sam. 25:13, 21f., 33f.), but it is the direction in which it was applied that is significant. As for David's 'ambush', we have only the word of the paranoid Saul for it, and paranoia is not a very likely source of historical information. Furthermore, what David might have done if he had been caught up in the conflict at Gilboa is one of the more intriguing side-issues of Israelite history, but we may as well confess that we know no more than the Philistine commanders (cf. 1 Sam. 29:3ff.), unless it be that David had been assiduously double-crossing Achish for some time (cf. 1 Sam. 27:8-12). The question of David's war with Eshbaal would have to be discussed in the light of his anointing as king by the men of Judah, his own tribe (2 Sam. 2:4), and of the responsibility that was thereby laid upon him. Saul had failed to meet his greatest challenge as king when he lost to the Philistines, Eshbaal was unexpectedly, and apparently inadequately, his successor, and the kingdom was willy-nilly divided in two. A charge of *lèse-majesté* against David will therefore simply not stand.

Ishida's charge that the author of the History 'doth protest too much' in the matter of David's innocence defies refutation by its own terms, but is entirely dependent on his arguments as outlined above. On the other hand, we have noted the existence of two accounts of David's sparing of Saul, in 1 Samuel 24 and 26. If these are independent reports of separate incidents, they are a double affirmative of David's innocence; if, as the majority of scholars aver, they are duplicates, then it is useful to recall that editors do not normally create duplicates; they inherit them.

Internal evidence for the dating of the History of David's Rise is non-existent, but attempts at establishing it have been made all the same. The fact that the 'Succession Narrative' appears to presuppose information given in the earlier narrative has influenced some scholars towards a tenth-century dating; however, the Solomonic dating of the Succession Narrative looks a lot less secure now than it did a few years ago. Some attempts at dating the History of David's Rise assume for it a strong propagandist role, whereby it was intended to justify David's conduct en route to the throne, particularly in the eyes of the Saulide faction which, all through his reign, was a thorn in his side (cf. 2 Sam. 16:5-13; 20:1-22). This apologia is therefore dated to the reign of Solomon, when the kingdom was as yet undivided and there remained a hope of holding it together. Ward, who finds in the History a fairly positive attitude towards the Saulides, suggests that it was prepared by a member of Solomon's court as the official version of David's early career. Crüsemann is substantially in agreement when he suggests a date in the latter part of David's reign or early in the reign of Solomon. Conrad and Mettinger, however, find a Solomonic dating unlikely in view of the possibility of an unfavourable contrast between Solomon, who established his rule by bloodshed, and the David of the History. It is an important point, especially since one of Solomon's victims was Shimei, from the same clan as Saul (1 Kgs 2:8f., 36-46; cf. 2 Sam. 16:5); though it could be countered that the executions of Joab and Shimei are said to have been carried out on the express advice of David (1 Kgs 2:5-9). Mettinger locates the History in the period immediately after Solomon's death, defining its purpose as the legitimation of 'the Davidic, Jerusalemite claims to total supremacy over "all Israel" after the dissolution of the personal union'. Grønbaek favours the reign of Baasha (c. 906-883 BC), while Conrad thinks that the History has northerners like the blood-letting Jehu (later ninth century) in mind.

Finally, in one of the most recent studies of the History, McCarter pushes the date of composition right back into the reign of David, on the ground that the very specific rebuttal of a number of charges to which David had left himself open would make most sense if David was still alive and likely to benefit personally from the exercise. Some justification for this view is found in H.A. Hoffner's comparison of the History of David's Rise with the Hittite 'Apology of Ḫattushilish' (13th century BC), which seeks to legitimize the rule of a king who had usurped his predecessor. Naturally, such a literary enterprise would tend to be undertaken in the lifetime of the king whose position was being defended! Hoffner suggests, moreover, that, even with its relative internal stability, the imperial Hittite kingdom managed to produce something akin to a 'tradition of royal apologies' dealing with this kind of situation. One notable feature shared by the History and the 'Apology of Hattushilish' is their emphasis on the divine patronage enjoyed by their respective protagonists. If the Hittite king can fulsomely attribute his successes to the goddess Ishtar, so our account of David reminds us at intervals—in what is frequently dignified as a *leitmotiv* of the History—that he succeeded because 'the LORD was with him' (e.g. 1 Sam. 16:18; 18:14; 2 Sam. 5:10).

So the History of David's Rise, however we define it, resists any suggestion that David's progress was achieved at the cost of Saulide blood. At the same time, skilful plot development and character portrayal ensure that the narrative does not decline into dull, monotonous apologetic. A key figure in this regard is Jonathan, Saul's eldest son, who, heedless of his own high expectations, assists David in the realization of his. While it would be unfair to dismiss Jonathan as merely a 'literary figure', the way in which he is introduced at moments of desperation and crisis for David gives him the air of a kindly genie. And, most importantly in a narrative which gives space to the theme of recognition, Jonathan is the first of the reigning house to acknowledge that David is destined for royal honours; already at 18:1-5, in the sequel to David's victory over Goliath, there is what may be described as Jonathan's 'virtual abdication' (cf. Jobling) when he hands over to David the tokens of his own princely status. It is, as the remainder of the story shows, an excellent piece of symbolism.

Further Reading

Of the several monographs devoted to the History of David's Rise only one is in English:

> R.L. Ward, *The Story of David's Rise: A Traditio-historical Study of I Samuel xvi 14—II Samuel v* (dissertation at Vanderbilt University, 1967; available from Univ. Microfilms, Ann Arbor).

Three monographs in German have also been influential, though the first two listed are unpublished dissertations:

H.-U. Nübel, *Davids Aufstieg in der frühe israelitischer Geschichts-schreibung* (diss. Bonn, 1959).

F. Mildenberger, *Die vordeuteronomistische Saul-Davidüberlieferung* (diss. Tübingen, 1962).

J.H. Grønbaek, *Die Geschichte vom Aufstieg Davids (1. Sam. 15–2. Sam. 5). Tradition und Komposition* (Acta Theologica Danica, 10), Copenhagen: Munksgaard, 1971.

Other relevant studies include:

A. Weiser, 'Die Legitimation des Königs David. Zur Eigenart und Entstehung der sogen. Geschichte von Davids Aufstieg', *VT* 16 (1966), 325-354.

J. Conrad, 'Zum geschichtlichen Hintergrund der Darstellung von Davids Aufstieg', *TLZ* 97 (1972), cols 321-332.

F. Schicklberger, 'Die Davididen und das Nordreich. Beobachtungen zur sog. Geschichte vom Aufstieg Davids', *BZ* NF 18 (1974), 255-263.

N.P. Lemche, 'David's Rise', *JSOT* 10 (1978), 2-25.

D. Jobling, 'Jonathan: A Structural Study in 1 Samuel', in *The Sense of Biblical Narrative* (*JSOT* Suppl., 7), Sheffield: JSOT Press, 1978, 4-25.

J.D. Levenson, '1 Samuel 25 as Literature and as History', *CBQ* 40 (1978), 11-28.

R.P. Gordon, 'David's Rise and Saul's Demise: Narrative Analogy in 1 Samuel 24-26', *TB* 31 (1980), 37-64.

J.C. VanderKam, 'Davidic Complicity in the Deaths of Abner and Eshbaal: A Historical and Redactional Study', *JBL* 99 (1980), 521-539.

R. North, 'David's Rise: Sacral, Military, or Psychiatric?', *Biblica* 63 (1982), 524-544.

Rost, 109-112.

Mettinger, 33-47.

Ishida, 55-63 (cf. 63-80).

J.A. Soggin, in Hayes—Miller, 333-335.

Gunn, *Saul*, 77-131.

Crüsemann, 128-142.

Political and apologetic aspects of the History of David's Rise are discussed in:

H.A. Hoffner, Jr, 'Propaganda and Political Justification in Hittite Historiography', in *Unity and Diversity: Essays in the History, Literature, and Religion of the Ancient Near East* (ed. H. Goedicke, J.J.M. Roberts), Baltimore/London: Johns Hopkins University Press, 1975, 49-62.

P.K. McCarter, Jr, 'The Apology of David', *JBL* 99 (1980), 489-504.

7

THE DAVIDIC
COVENANT
(2 SAMUEL 7)

R ISING somewhat above the imponderabilia of the boundary limits of the History of David's Rise and the Succession Narrative, 2 Samuel 7 has an importance all its own as presenting the classic expression of the royal Davidic ideology of ancient Israel. The chapter relates how David, having declared his intention of erecting a permanent shrine for God, received a divine assurance which embraced not merely the building of the temple—to be entrusted, in any case, to his son and successor—but also the prospect of an enduring Davidic dynasty. While the word 'covenant' does not appear in the chapter, there is sufficient ancillary covenant terminology throughout to endorse its use in the key texts which comment on this oracle, viz. 2 Samuel 23:5, Psalm 89:3, 28, 34, and Psalm 132:12. We are, then, in the world of promissory covenant in 2 Samuel 7.

Literary analysis has produced very diverse results when practised on this chapter. There are those who have argued for literary unity, whether in the interests of an aetiological hypothesis, or on the basis of comparisons with the Egyptian *Königsnovelle* ('king's novel'), or on the assumption of Deuteronomistic composition, but the prevailing tendency is to discover a more complex literary history. Herrmann's comparison with the *Königsnovelle*, which records Pharaonic decisions announced to courtiers in audience, was for a time influential in promoting the unitary view, but even Herrmann himself has to confess to an occasional contortion in order to make the parallels match. In what follows, only a representative sampling of the numerous analyses of 2 Samuel 7 can be given.

Rost identified verses 11b and 16 as the core of the original dynastic oracle, and tentatively dated these, together with verses 1-7, 18-21, 25-29, to the reign of David. Further stages in the development of the chapter were marked by the inclusion of the more specific references to

David's successor, as well as of some other verses, in the time of Isaiah
(vv. 8-11a, 12, 14, 15, 17), by the Deuteronomistic addition of verse
13a in Josiah's reign, and by the insertion of verses 22-24 during the
exilic period. This recognition of a basic dynastic promise which was
supplemented at some point by 'Solomonic' additions has proved an
acceptable workinᵧ hypothesis for a number of scholars, but it has
been challenged by Mettinger, who thinks it unlikely that an oracle of
dynastic compass would subsequently be reduced to the level of an
oracle of succession. By reversing the process, therefore, Mettinger
postulates two pre-Deuteronomistic layers, one consisting of verses
1a, 2-7, 12-14a, 16 (as LXX), 17, and dated to Solomon's reign, the other
('the dynastic redaction') comprising verses 8, 9, 11b, 14b, 15f., 18-22a,
27-29 and introduced soon after Solomon's death in order to extend the
applicability of the Solomonic promise to the whole house of David.

Veijola recognized two separate oracles in verses 1a, 2-5, 7, and
verses 8a, 9f., 12, 14, 15, 17, dealing with the issues of temple-building
and of David's immediate successor respectively. Under the influence
of Deuteronomistic redaction, says Veijola, the temple ceased to be
regarded as the dwelling-place of God in the immanent sense, and the
promise relating to David's successor was expanded into a dynastic
oracle. Ishida, by contrast, limits himself to the suggestion that, in
Solomon's reign, either Nathan or his sons composed the bulk of 2
Samuel 7 from prophetic utterances of Nathan delivered to David on a
number of separate occasions. 'From the parallel of the collections of
prophecies in the royal archives at Mari and Nineveh, we may infer
that Nathan's prophecies were also preserved as a collection in the
royal archive in Jerusalem. In this way, the prophecies which Nathan
had made to David were reinterpreted for the legitimation of Solomon.'

Compared with the diverse results of the above-mentioned literary-
critical studies—and it must be stressed that we have taken only the
merest sampling from a large field—Ishida's approach produces the
kind of holistic appraisal which the chapter seems to merit. There is a
literary and thematic unity which is attributable in no small way to the
vertebral occurrences of 'house' throughout the chapter (vv. 1, 2, 5, 6,
7, 11, 13, 16, 18, 19, 25, 26, 27, 29); it is 'house', in one or other of its
senses, which binds together the apparently unrelated topics of David's
building a temple for God and God's establishing a dynasty for David
(cf. vv. 5ff., 11). Nevertheless, as Ishida observes, the conjoining of the
themes of temple and dynasty is not peculiar to 2 Samuel 7 among the
texts of the ancient near east.

Verses 1-7. David's proposal to build a temple follows on naturally from the account, in the previous chapter, of the installation of the ark of the covenant in a tent in Jerusalem. Furthermore, in near eastern reckoning Yahweh's victories over the enemies of Israel, executed through David and issuing in the 'rest' of verse 1, qualified him to have a shrine worthy of his accomplishments—just as, in the oft-quoted Ugaritic text, Baal, through Anath, petitions El for a 'house' following his defeat of Yam. As is evident from the rare instances of the gods' rejection of temple-building proposals in Mesopotamian literature, such a refusal would be regarded as a snub and a setback, so that it is hard to envisage a Hebrew writer fictionalizing about God's, and Nathan's, opposition, if there was not already a tradition of a prophetic oracle expressed in these terms. Cross, indeed, finds an underlying poetic structure in verse 2, a couplet which he thinks may go back to the time of David.

Why, then, was David forbidden to build the temple? And are we to construe verses 1-7 as an outright rejection of the temple concept? On the assumption of an originally unqualified rejection, several answers have been proposed, such as that the building of a temple was an encroachment upon Israel's older sacral institutions, or that Nathan's veto was a diplomatic attempt to ease prevailing political tensions in Jerusalem. Others relate the interdict more closely to David's personal aspirations, as if he was setting himself up as one of those oriental despots whose wont was to crown their secular achievements with religious undertakings of this sort. In this connection von Nordheim fairly remarks that David would have done little for the ark of the covenant with his temple-building, but the ark would have done a lot for him. But even if this represents a judicious reading between the lines, we have to allow that the biblical text speaks of God's desire to enhance David's glory as if David's intention had been transparently honourable from the outset.

It is important, nonetheless, to observe that verses 1-7 do not convey a final rejection of the proposal to build a temple. Carlson, with parenthetical references to his Scandinavian mentors, explains with admirable succinctness: 'The situation is rather that the passage 7:5b-7 described the period of the Ark's sojourn in the tabernacle as a "period of unrest and wandering" (Pedersen), thus placing the following period in perspective; in this way the years still remaining before Solomon's building can be represented as tolerable (Mowinckel)'. Thus, while it is true that the section begins with the statement that 'the LORD had given him [David] rest from all his enemies', it is, from the perspective of the chapter as a whole, an incomplete rest. This is particularly clear from the use of the future tense in verses 9b-11a, where we might have expected the past. Here the point is made that, even after all David's achievements, there is a level of security and prosperity to which the kingdom has not yet attained—there is a 'rest' which, according to verse 11, is still future. Seen from this standpoint, even the Shiloh temple does not merit mention as a 'house' (cf. vv. 6f.), since it is associated with the period of 'unrest'. It may also be significant that this chapter is followed by a summary of David's conquests in 8:1-14, as if to underline the proposition that 'rest' is a relative term in 7:1. Solomon's message to Hiram of Tyre in 1 Kings 5:3f. certainly expresses this view: 'You know that David my father could not build a house for the name of the LORD his God because of the warfare with which his enemies surrounded him, until the LORD put them under the soles of his feet. But now the LORD my God has given me rest on every side; there is neither adversary nor misfortune.'

Some, willing to discover a redactional link between verses 1-7 and the main oracle in verses 8-17, distinguish between the function of the temple as a divine dwelling, in verses 5f., and as a place where God's name is honoured, in verse 13 ('for my name'). According to this view, the 'name theology' of verse 13 represents a refinement of the more localized conception of God's dwelling in verses 5f.; this then explains how David's plan is turned down and yet the building of the temple in the next reign is considered acceptable. Carlson, however, plays down this supposed distinction, incompatible as it is with his views on the Deuteronomistic composition of 2 Samuel. He notes that the 'dwelling' was intended to house the ark of the covenant, and claims that 'for my dwelling' in verse 5b is just a Deuteronomistic variant of the more usual 'for my name' (as v. 13a). Quite apart from the text-critical question—in verse 13 the not unimportant Lucianic strand in the Septuagint tradition has, like the parallel text in 1 Chronicles 17:12, 'for me' instead of 'for my name'—uncertainty about the significance of the Deuteronomistic 'name theology' and the laconicism with which the idea is expressed in MT of verse 13 counsel against too facile a distinction; to that extent Carlson has a point.

Verses 8-17. One of the outstanding features of the kingdom of Judah was the stability of its throne; apart from the six years when Athaliah held sway, after the death of her son Ahaziah (cf. 2 Kgs 11:1-3), the land was ruled by the house of David right down to the

Babylonian captivity. Not even when its failings assumed monumental proportions could that house cease to be the focus of national hope, and its rulers 'the breath of our nostrils' (Lam. 4:20). That dynastic 'lamp' (cf. 1 Kgs 11:36) was fuelled by an oracle delivered to David by the prophet Nathan and recorded in these verses.

We have already seen that the oracle has been variously treated by a large number of scholars, but, however it is analyzed, verses 11b and 16 appear to constitute the core. In that Rost spoke rightly. Apart from the flash-back in verses 8-9a, the rest relates to Solomon and the conditions of his reign (for vv. 9b-11a see above). That which pertains to the promise of a perpetual Davidic dynasty, viz. verses 11b and 16, is characterized as an 'everlasting covenant' in 2 Samuel 23:5, in a verse section which is of prime importance because of its widely acknowledged contemporaneity with David. It is with some justification, therefore, that the Nathan oracle has been drawn into the orbit of the near eastern vassal treaty, for example by Calderone, who begins with the premiss that the near east knows of no instance of a god promising to maintain a whole dynasty, and proceeds to supply the desiderated analogy from the so-called 'vassal' or 'suzerainty' treaty, in which the military overlord customarily undertook to ensure the stability of the local ruling house, provided that the treaty obligations imposed upon it were met. Calderone's comparisons are almost all with the second millennium Hittite treaties—which, whatever the pros and cons of thus restricting the survey, at least enables him to compare the retrospective comment of verses 8-9a with the historical introduction which was a feature of the ancient vassal treaty, and which is better attested in the Hittite than in the extant neo-Assyrian texts. The vassal treaty analogy might also illuminate the disciplinary clauses in verses 14f., for although the point of such treaty provisions often was that an insubordinate vassal would forfeit his limited sovereignty, it may be that in this case a deliberate contrast is being drawn (see especially v. 15a). In a general way, too, the recognized compatibility of the covenant and treaty concepts in the Old Testament domain could be cited in support of the treaty analogy in 2 Samuel 7.

But there have been attempts to shed light on the Nathan oracle from other near eastern sources, and to these we briefly turn. Important points of comparison between the oracle and the Hittite and Assyrian 'royal grants' have been noted by Weinfeld. In the 'royal grant' the king makes a gift of land to a servant as a reward for loyal service rendered. David, then, as the loyal servant of Yahweh was rewarded with an assurance of a perpetual dynasty, in a covenant undertaking which, as we shall shortly see, did not lack a land dimension.

A third possibility is suggested by Ishida, who finds the principal elements of 2 Samuel 7, including David's prayer in verses 18-29, paralleled in building inscriptions from the temple sites of Mesopotamia. Complementary evidence in the form of neo-Assyrian prophecies—specifically, a collection of prophecies addressed to Esarhaddon and Ashurbanipal—exhibiting similar features, though without reference to temple-building, is also adduced. In fact, Ishida concludes that 'Nathan's prophecy resembles the Neo-Assyrian prophecies much more closely than the Egyptian royal novel both in themes and in the relation of the king to the god'. On the basis of yet other texts Ishida explains the lord-servant relationship between God and David in 2 Samuel 7, not in terms of the suzerain-vassal relationships of the treaties, but of the tutelary deity and his dynasty. This, he thinks, is what is implied in 2 Samuel 23:5 ('my house is with God').

Finally, we note Malamat's claim that the second (published) letter from eighteenth-century Mari contains a 'dynastic oracle', albeit with the difference that Adad's promise to Zimri-lim is of the conditional type. As it happens, we need not restrict ourselves to any one of these comparisons, in view of what has been called the 'functional and formal overlap' between one type of text and another. A shared ideology and common drafting techniques mean that even boundary inscriptions and treaty texts may exhibit formal and conceptual similarities over a wide area in the ancient near east.

One of the most remarkable features of Nathan's oracle is the statement that God would initiate Solomon into a father-son relationship with himself. Rost dated verses 14f., where this idea is expressed, to the time of Isaiah; but the extra-biblical evidence would not suggest that the concept itself was a late-comer to Israel—witness, for example, the kingship ideology of Ugarit in the second millennium. The divine sonship of the king was also integral to Egyptian kingship ideology, though with the important distinction that the pharaoh was held to be literally a son of the god. By contrast, the Israelite king was 'son' in a non-mythological, adoptive or legitimizing, sense, being 'adopted' at his coronation into a unique relationship with God, as both his confidant and his vice-gerent on earth.

Various aspects of 2 Samuel 7 point to the Davidic covenant as a reflex of the Abrahamic covenant described in Genesis 15. That there should have been interaction between the two covenant traditions would follow as a natural corollary from the recognition of the Davidic kingdom as in some way fulfilling the promises made to Abraham. According to one suggestion, that development may be traced to David's period of rule from Hebron (cf. 2 Sam. 2:1-4; 3:2-5; 5:1-5), a city with an honourable place in the Abrahamic tradition. This relationship, as of promise and fulfilment, between the two covenants is signalled in the corresponding references to 'name' (2 Sam. 7:9 // Gen. 12:2) and 'seed' (2 Sam. 7:12 // Gen. 15:3f.), and is made even more explicit in connection with the reign of Solomon when 'Judah and Israel were as many as the sand by the sea' (1 Kgs 4:20 // Gen. 22:17; 32:12), and Solomon 'ruled over all the kingdoms from the Euphrates to the land of the Philistines and to the border of Egypt' (1 Kgs 4:21 // Gen. 15:18-21).

Verses 18-29. David's prayer, as has often been remarked, makes no mention of the building of the temple, centring, rather, on the dynastic promise. In verses 22-24 the covenant is seen as having significance for the whole people of Israel, who form the third party in a covenantal trio consisting of Yahweh, the house of David, and Israel. In this way the national covenant of Sinai is both fulfilled and superseded as Israel receives a means of grace in its ruling house and through that house participates in a covenant relationship which is not bounded by conditions. Some, moreover, discover broader horizons in the words 'and this is the law of men' in verse 19, the clause being interpreted to mean that the Davidic covenant has implications for all mankind; but the Hebrew is cryptic and the quotation in 1 Chronicles 17:17 substantially different. There are better Old Testament texts for such a sermon (e.g. Is. 55).

The Nathan oracle represents a peak in the books of Samuel and in the Old Testament as a whole. The earlier chapters of 1 and 2 Samuel are punctuated with anticipatory references to it (e.g. 1 Sam. 13:13f.; 20:15; 24:20; 25:28; 2 Sam. 3:9f.; 5:12; 6:21), and thereafter it reaches on into the psalms and prophecies in the remainder of the Hebrew canon, 'the climax of the narrative which precedes it and the program for what follows' (McCarthy, adapted). And so, when Judah was desolate and its king an exile in Babylon, it seems that the invincibility of the Davidic hope enabled a Jew, probably himself living in Babylonia, to discover in the release of Jehoiachin from prison a hint of the possible resurrection of the house of David (2 Kgs

25:27-30). That too was the hope of the prophets Haggai and
Zechariah who preached in the period immediately following the
return from Babylon (cf. Hg. 2:20-23).

By virtue of the explicit word which it contains, the Nathan oracle
represents 'the historical origin and legitimation of all messianic
expectations' (von Rad, *Old Testament Theology* I, 311). But of
scarcely less importance is the fact that its operative force was in
inverse proportion to the capacity for fulfilment of the ideal shown by
the weak Davidic scions who succeeded one another on David's
throne in Jerusalem. As the monarchy sank into decline, with but few
hints of restorative vigour, the discrepancy between the ideal and the
reality both made the ideal more remote and the conviction about its
realization more certain—more remote in that the depiction of the
glories of the expected Davidic king far exceeded the record of the
historical David; more certain, since under no circumstances could
the enfeebled house of David be said to have fulfilled the prophetic
expectation. When the earliest Christian community identified Jesus
of Nazareth as the promised offspring of David it took over the rich
store of Old Testament references to David's house and its glorious
future. The extent to which this took place can be gathered from the
use made of 2 Samuel 7:14 in Hebrews 1:5, where 'I will be to him a
father, and he shall be to me a son' now concerns not Solomon but
the incarnate Son. And, in similar fashion, the writer builds up his
catena of Old Testament texts, some originally expressive of Davidic
ideology—notably Psalms 2:7, 45:6f., 110:1—to support his argument
that Christ as 'Son' is superior even to angels.

Further Reading

On the importance of the dynastic oracle for the Deuteronomistic History as
a whole see:

D.J. McCarthy, 'II Samuel 7 and the Structure of the Deuteronomic
History', *JBL* 84 (1965), 131-138.

Cross, *CMHE*, 229-237, 241-264.

For discussion of the relationship between the Abrahamic and the Davidic
covenants see:

R.E. Clements, *Abraham and David. Genesis 15 and its meaning for
Israelite Tradition* (SBT, II/5), Geneva, Al.: Allenson-
Breckinridge / London: SCM Press, 1967, 47-60.

N.E. Wagner, 'Abraham and David?', in *Studies on the Ancient Palestinian World* (Fs F.V. Winnett; Toronto Semitic Texts and Studies, 2; ed. J.W. Wevers, D.B. Redford), Toronto: University of Toronto Press, 1972, 117-140.

Comparisons with other near eastern texts are made in the following:

i. *Egyptian*

S. Herrmann, 'Die Königsnovelle in Ägypten und in Israel', *Wissenschaftliche Zeitschrift der Universität Leipzig* 3 (1953-4), 51-62.

M. Görg, *Gott-König-Reden in Israel und Ägypten* (BWANT, 105), Stuttgart: Kohlhammer, 1975, 178-271.

ii. *Mari prophetic texts*

A. Malamat, 'Prophetic Revelations in New Documents from Mari and the Bible', *VTS* 15 (1966), 207-227.

Malamat, 'A Mari Prophecy and Nathan's Dynastic Oracle', in *Prophecy* (Fs G. Fohrer; BZAW, 150; ed. J.A. Emerton), Berlin/New York: Walter de Gruyter, 1980, 68-82.

iii. *Land grants*

M. Weinfeld, 'The Covenant of Grant in the Old Testament and in the Ancient Near East', *JAOS* 90 (1970), 184-203.

Weinfeld, *Deuteronomy*, 74-81 (see bibliography to Chapter 1).

Weinfeld, in Botterweck—Ringgren, II, 270-272.

iv. *Vassal treaties*

P.J. Calderone, *Dynastic Oracle and Suzerainty Treaty. 2 Samuel 7, 8-16* (Logos, 1), Manila: Ateneo University Publications, 1966.

On the 'law of men' (2 Sam. 7:19b) see:

O. Eissfeldt, *Kleine Schriften* (ed. R. Sellheim, F. Maass), V, Tübingen: J.C.B. Mohr (Paul Siebeck), 1973, 143-151.

W.C. Kaiser, Jr, 'The Blessing of David: The Charter for Humanity', in *The Law and the Prophets* (Fs O.T. Allis; ed. J.H. Skilton), Nutley: Presbyterian and Reformed Press, 1974, 298-318.

Other useful discussions of 2 Samuel 7 may be found in:

E. von Nordheim, 'König und Tempel. Der Hintergrund des Tempelbauverbotes in 2 Samuel vii', *VT* 27 (1977), 434-453.

M. Tsevat, 'The Steadfast House: What was David Promised in 2 Samuel 7?', in *The Meaning of the Book of Job and Other Biblical Studies. Essays on the Literature and Religion of the Hebrew Bible*, New York: Ktav, 1980, 101-117 (= *HUCA* 34 [1963], 71-82).

Rost, 35-56.

Carlson, 106-128.

Mettinger, 48-63.

Ishida, 81-117.

Veijola, *Dynastie*, 68-79.

8

THE SUCCESSION NARRATIVE

'From things like Noah's Ark or the sun standing still upon Ajalon, you come down to the court memoirs of King David.' (C.S. Lewis, 'Is Theology Poetry?')

THE OTHER leaf of Rost's Davidic 'diptych' is 'the matchless "History of the Throne Succession"' (J. Bright), not indeed discovered by Rost, but owing its classic exposition to him. This narrative, comprising 2 Samuel 9-20 and 1 Kings 1-2, as well as certain verses culled from 2 Samuel 6-7, was, according to Rost, set in the key of 1 Kings 1:20: 'And now, my lord the king, the eyes of all Israel are upon you, to tell them who shall sit on the throne of my lord the king after him'. It was, then, in the strict sense a narrative of *succession*.

1. **Boundaries**

With respect to its beginning and ending the Succession Narrative exhibits the same elusive qualities as the Ark Narrative and the History of David's Rise. Rost thought 2 Samuel 9:1 an unlikely start to the Succession Narrative and found more promising material in 6:16, 20-23, which verses treat of Michal, Saul's daughter and David's wife, and of the barrenness which scotched any hope of Davidide and Saulide loyalties converging on one of her offspring. (This point was taken up by von Rad, who saw 6:23, which notes Michal's infertility, answered in the new possibilities of the dynastic oracle of ch. 7.) Rost also reckoned that a short version of the Nathan oracle of 2 Samuel 7, viz. the 'core' consisting of verses 11b and 16, formed part of the original Narrative. Mettinger is not averse to this suggestion, though he finds the evidence inconclusive. He is also quite favourably disposed towards the view, espoused by Carlson, that 2 Samuel 21:1-14, relating the execution of seven of Saul's family, once stood in front of 2 Samuel 9.

A more radical approach to this question is adopted by D.M. Gunn in his monograph *The Story of King David*. Gunn makes a strong case for including not only the verses in 2 Samuel 6, but also the greater part of 2 Samuel 2-4, on the grounds that, first, these chapters provide the background to David's question in 9:1, that, secondly, without them Abner alone of the various characters mentioned in 1 Kings 2 would be making his début at that point, and that, thirdly, stylistically they align themselves with the Succession Narrative. The Nathan oracle, however, is 'ideologically obvious and tediously repetitive' and is judged unworthy of a place in the Narrative!

Fewer problems attend the discussion of the far limit of the Narrative, since there is no possibility of its extending beyond 1 Kings 2. 1 Kings 3, which begins with Solomon's dream at Gibeon, takes us into different territory. The Succession Narrative therefore concludes with the kingdom established in Solomon's hand, whether we put a full stop at 2:46 with Rost, or at 2:12 with a number of others. Rost denominated several sentences in ch. 2 (vv. 3f., 11, 27b) as secondary additions to the Narrative—a restrained attempt at pruning compared with the work of later seasons. The whole of 2:13-46(46a) is pronounced 'secondary' by, among others, Noth, Gray, and Mettinger, the latter also putting 1:41-53 in this class. However, as Rost had already noted, the excision of 1:41-53 is particularly ill-advised because it leaves the account of Adonijah's rebellion hanging in the air, with no indication given as to what finally befell Adonijah.

Again the mere recital of a few representative views on the zoning of a hypothetical entity like the Succession Narrative raises basic questions as to what kind of text it is with which we are working. It is hard not to sympathize with Carlson, who frankly says that the Narrative is too thoroughly integrated into Samuel—Kings, and contains too much in the nature of recollection and foreshadowing, to be separable from the rest. As an example of 'recollection' Carlson quotes the Mephibosheth story in 2 Samuel 9, with its obvious dependence upon 1 Samuel 20; 23:17f.; 24:8-22. Here, too, the question of thematic and verbal interplay between narratives within and without the supposed 'source' deserves mention. For instance, there is sufficient interplay between 2 Samuel 20:14-22 and 21:1-6, and especially in the verbal correspondences between 20:19 and 21:2f., to raise doubts as to whether it can be simply adventitious. Henceforth in this chapter, therefore, the term 'Succession Narrative' will be used to denote 2 Samuel 9-20; 1 Kings 1-2 without prejudice to the question of the independent status of the Narrative.

2. Genre

The Succession Narrative envisaged by Rost was an account of David's reign extending to Solomon's accession, proximate to the events described, and perhaps even making use of eyewitness reports. (Rost reckoned that the developed Davidic idealism of later centuries would not have permitted so candid a portrait of David as is presented in the Narrative.) This became a 'received tradition' which was faithfully retailed in most discussions of Samuel—Kings, for example in Bright's *A History of Israel* ('a document with an eyewitness flavor which can hardly have been written many years after Solomon succeeded to the throne'). Gerhard von Rad hailed the Narrative as one of the two great Israelite historical works—the other was the Yahwistic history—produced in the period of the so-called 'Solomonic Enlightenment', a time when, as he thought, a fresh understanding of the relationship between God and history was hammered out. But increasingly it is being asked whether contemporaneity is a necessary corollary of the 'eyewitness' impression created by the Narrative, and whether, indeed, it is not being miscalled when it is classified as 'history', since some of the connotations of that term are not applicable to ancient Semitic historiography.

Eissfeldt, a born sceptic where the Samuel 'narratives' are concerned, had already queried the right of the private scenes, of which the rape of Tamar in 2 Samuel 13 is an obvious example, to be regarded as historical in the strict sense. And we can easily appreciate why such a narrative should depend on something other than first-hand reportage. More general criticisms of the 'historical' character of the Narrative, now not concerned so much with facticity as with its concept of history, have also been made. In the first instance, there is the narrative's apparent independence of external sources, the one exception being the account of the Ammonite War (10:1–11:1; 12:26–31). The Narrative has also been faulted for its lack of interest in the more broadly political aspects of David's reign, as exemplified in its failure to analyse the causes of the discontent which enabled Absalom to drive his father into temporary exile from Jerusalem: the major 'historical event' described in the Narrative is, to a remarkable degree, treated as family history. Of course, the absence of references to underlying sources becomes noteworthy only if there is a significant gap between the event and the retelling of the same; a contemporary or near-contemporary writer would not have recourse to sources in the same way as someone writing several generations later. Moreover, the preoccupation of the Narrative with personalia could be seen as arising out of the understandable interest and concern of someone familiar with the times which he is describing. But these arguments rest too heavily on a Solomonic dating for the Narrative to be aired with much conviction, and, whereas the domesticity of the Narrative is really only a liability when the succession theme is discounted, it is manifestly true that its author is not aiming to provide his readers with a political perspective on David's reign. To that extent it is a 'court history'. But it is a reflective 'court history' in which the author displays a keen interest in human psychology and, despite his aversion to political analysis, some awareness of historical causation.

There have been other assessments of the Narrative which, while not denying the presence of historical elements, describe its primary function in non-historical terms. Several writers have associated it with the Israelite 'wisdom circles' among which the values and modes of expression and instruction represented in the wisdom books of the Old Testament were fostered. Whybray, in attributing to the Narrative the dual role of propagandist novel and manual of wisdom instruction, compares various Egyptian texts, from the second millennium BC, in which these two interests are combined, and in particular the 'Instruction of Amenemhet', because of the parallel which he sees between David, founder of the Judaean dynasty, and Amenemhet, founder of the Egyptian Twelfth Dynasty. Crüsemann also traces the Narrative to courtly wisdom circles, but for him it presents a wise man's critique of kingship comparable with the various instructions to kings in the book of Proverbs. The Succession Narrative, says Crüsemann, illustrates the good effect of criticism on a king and contains a message for Solomon who, if he follows the example of his father, will benefit in the same way.

Another alternative to 'history' and 'wisdom manual' as generic descriptions of the Narrative is preferred by D.M. Gunn who invokes the concept of 'story' which has usefully been applied to various parts of the Old Testament. For Gunn the Narrative functions pre-eminently as (serious) entertainment. The chief objection which he raises to its classification as 'history' is that it is too dependent on traditional motifs such as the judgment-eliciting parable (2 Sam. 12, 14), or the woman and the spies (2 Sam. 17), to pass as straightforward factual narration, though he allows that there may be real events and persons behind the story ('stories based on historical incidents can be subject to reshaping in tradition while yet retaining for teller and audience the character of "truth"'"). Gunn's use of the term 'traditional composition' has, it is true, been criticized by van Seters, but Gunn maintains his position in the third chapter of his 1978 volume.

3. Theme

Hamlet without the Prince of Denmark?

The Succession Narrative adumbrated in, for example, Wellhausen's work and advocated by Rost was principally, as its name suggests, a narrative of *succession*, tracing 'the steps by which Solomon, whose birth, with its attendant circumstances, is narrated at the outset, reached the throne over the heads of his brothers Amnon, Absalom, and Adonijah, who stood before him' (J. Wellhausen, *Prolegomena*, 262). Since there is the briefest of references to Solomon in 2 Samuel 12, and he does not make his entrance proper until 1 Kings 1, this means that the hero of the story is introduced only after the rival claimants to the throne have disqualified themselves in one way or another. For some this invisibility of the hero for so much of the narrative constitutes a fundamental objection to the recognition of the Narrative as a document principally about either Solomon or the issue of succession. J.W. Flanagan simply evacuates it of the Solomonic sections, viz. 2 Samuel 11:2–12:25—which fills in the background to the birth of Solomon—and 1 Kings 1-2, and treats the remainder as a 'Court History'. Exit the prince of Denmark! The addition of the Solomonic sections is attributed by Flanagan to 'a skillful redactor'. This, however, smacks too much of the anti-thesis, for even if we were to concede that 1 Kings 1-2 is a later addition, and one which converts the torso of the 'Court History' into a narrative of succession, there is no reason why Solomon should go altogether unmentioned in such a 'Court History'. It would be a singularly unforeseeing 'Court History' which managed to avoid all reference to the particular son of David who actually did manage to succeed his father on the throne.

Gunn also opposes the Rostian definition of the theme of the Succession Narrative, for the reason that Rost let his conception of the theme determine the boundaries of the narrative. If, however, the bulk of 2 Samuel 2-4 is included in the Narrative, as Gunn claims it should be, then the cherished succession theme is demonstrably incapable of fulfilling the integrating role commonly ascribed to it.

By itself the succession 'theme' does not 'convey a clear sense of significant development or direction in the narrative or constitute the primary source of any dramatic tension'. Solomon is one of the least substantial figures in the Narrative and his coronation is an unexpected ending to the story, not its climax. In 2 Samuel 2–1 Kings 2 we have, according to Gunn, a story about King David, in whom alone all the various episodes, movements, and interests cohere. Similar misgivings about the importance of the succession theme are expressed by Conroy on the basis of a structural examination of 2 Samuel 13-20, a 'relatively independent narrative unit' which deserves to be read without prejudice from 1 Kings 1-2. Conroy holds that, if these chapters are really suffused with the succession theme, this should be evident even when they are taken in isolation from the rest of the Narrative. But he finds no evidence that they are: 'The question "Who will sit on David's throne after him?" is nowhere audible on the immediate text level of 2 Samuel 13-20'.

With an invisible hero and a barely audible question, the case for treating 2 Samuel 9-20 + 1 Kings 1-2 as first and foremost a narrative of succession might seem hardly to exist at all, even when due weight has been given to such references as 2 Samuel 14:7 ('the heir') and 1 Kings 1:6 ('next after Absalom'). Nor will appeal to the celebrated attributes of spareness, laconicism, and implicitness in Hebrew narrative really suffice to justify Rost's characterization of these chapters as a 'Succession Narrative'. The events described certainly have a bearing on the succession question, but this is not the primary motivation of the narrative. Only a theme formulated in terms of David himself is capable of accommodating the diverse episodes and interests of the Succession Narrative.

4. Tendenz

Until the publication of Delekat's essay in 1967, a seldom-contested corollary of the Succession Narrative hypothesis was that the chapters in question displayed a pro-Davidic and pro-Solomonic slant. Delekat, however, taking the Bathsheba episode as his starting-point, marshalled a fair amount of evidence in support of the contrary position, viz. that the Narrative regarded both David and Solomon with some disfavour. While, however, Delekat's shifting from pole to pole initiated a new phase in the debate, the tendency has been to recognize the presence in the Narrative of elements both for and against David and Solomon, and, in a few cases, to explain the supposed anomaly along redaction-critical lines. The principal names here are Würthwein, Veijola, and Langlamet. Würthwein, for example, devotes his second chapter to a discussion of the anti-Solomonic *Tendenz* of 1 Kings 1-2 and his third to anti-Davidic aspects of 2 Samuel 10-12, thereafter adducing evidence of a pro-Davidic/pro-Solomonic redaction of the original narrative. Veijola, building on the three-edition theory of the Deuteronomistic History advanced by W. Dietrich in 1972 (see Chapter 1), distinguishes between the original version, which showed David in a favourable light, and a later prophetic redaction which denied that there was any future for the Davidic house. The third ('nomistic') redactor was more favourably disposed towards David and depicted him as a man who lived in submission to the law of Yahweh. Langlamet, who concentrates on 1 Kings 1-2 in his first two articles, rigorously distinguishes between pro- and anti- Solomonic elements in the text in a manner that recalls the worst excesses of the earlier Pentateuchal critics. Indeed, this tendency to textual fission is one of the most serious weaknesses in the redaction-critical approach. Another is the underlying assumption that ancient writers, incapable of balancing preference with candour, were habitually in the grip of partisanship when they wrote of the events and personages of the national history. But we are entitled to ask whether a writer who has, in the case of the minor figures Mephibosheth and Ziba, so successfully managed to leave motive shrouded and loyalty ambiguous, was incapable of producing a frank account of the human strengths and foibles that were as characteristic of David and Solomon as of most other human beings. Even a propagandist undertaking need not degenerate into a whitewash.

At the same time as the redaction-critics were wielding their scalpels, Mettinger was restating the Rostian view that the Succession Narrative is unambiguously pro-Solomonic in outlook. Mettinger, who pursues his own private redactional venture in 1 Kings 1-2, argues that the Narrative was composed in order to exculpate Solomon from the most incriminating of the political executions carried out during his long reign, viz. those recorded in 1 Kings 2. Again the theory seems to depend for its vitality on the Solomonic dating of the Narrative, a question which we shall soon have to discuss.

5. Theology

It has been claimed that, whereas the earlier Israelite view of history was of a series of divine irruptions into the human scene, the Succession Narrative represents a new conception of history in which divine immanence and horizontal causality are the key factors. In von Rad's words, God's activity is 'concealed in the whole breadth of secular affairs, and pervading every single sphere of human life'. This representation of the Succession Narrative is largely inspired by the paucity of direct references to the involvement of God in the events which it describes; usually three only are cited, viz. 2 Samuel 11:27, 12:24, and 17:14. At the same time, von Rad was able to put things more in perspective with his observation that each of these statements marks a turning-point in the story. 2 Samuel 11:27 strikes an ominous note with regard to David's future and that of his family, while 12:24—especially when seen in the fuller light of day—by announcing God's approval of Solomon virtually proclaims his election as David's successor. Then in 17:14 the decisive turn in the Absalom rebellion is attributed to God's frustration of Ahithophel's exceedingly pertinent advice to Absalom; thereafter the rebel cause was as good as lost, and so obviously so that Ahithophel tidied up his affairs and committed suicide (17:23).

But there are other references to God's involvement in human affairs, and a balanced account of the theology of the Succession Narrative will not overlook them. Divine action is also noted, for example, in 2 Samuel 12:1, 15, and 1 Kings 2:15. The references to God's attitude and activity in relation to the Bathsheba episode (11:27; 12:1, 15) are especially significant, since they set in motion the series of upheavals and disasters which afflict the royal house throughout much of the remainder of 2 Samuel. Within the speeches there is, too, a class of utterances which uses the language of traditional piety (e.g. 2 Sam. 14:14; 15:8, 25; 16:12), and which is probably reflective, to a degree, of the 'theology' of the Narrative.

Another supposedly distinctive feature of the Succession Narrative is its indifference to cultic matters, this in contrast to the History of David's Rise, which has David regularly seeking oracular guidance from God (cf. 1 Sam. 22:10; 23:2, 4; 30:8; 2 Sam. 2:1; 5:19, 23). In the Succession Narrative the ark of the covenant and the oracular ephod play a minor role. It might even be claimed on the basis of 2 Samuel 11:11 ('The ark and Israel and Judah dwell in booths') and 2 Samuel

15:24ff. (David sends the ark back to Jerusalem) that the Narrative is teaching that God's favour can be enjoyed independently of the ark. Such an idea could, possibly, be extracted from the second passage, but scarcely from the first, for the ark's presence in the Israelite camp is to ensure victory, just as when it was taken to Ebenezer in 1 Samuel 4. Carlson detects an allusion to the ark in 2 Samuel 12:16 ('David therefore besought God for the child; and David fasted, and went in and lay all night upon the ground'), yet it is not clear that this act of prostration was performed in a shrine. However, what are we to make of 2 Samuel 16:23 in relation to this claimed secularity of the Succession Narrative? If the counsel of Ahithophel is said to have been as reliable as the divine oracle, then the ultimate standard of measurement must be the divine oracle!

There is also, in all probability, a literary dimension to this question of the alleged secularity of the Succession Narrative, since there is evidence of what Conroy describes as 'a new mastery of the art of narrative', involving less explication of theme, without, in this case, the adoption of a new theological stance: 'in a story the narrator can surely convey his stand-point just as well by his arrangement of the action and dialogue as by explicit thematic statements'. The juxtaposition of verses 31 and 32 in 2 Samuel 15 is a good illustration of what Conroy has in mind.

6. Date

The main arguments in favour of a Solomonic dating of the Narrative are usually considered to be: (i) the impression of contemporaneity which its vivid and detailed descriptions create, and (ii) the improbability that the developed Davidic idealism of later generations would have permitted so frank a portrayal of David. These are, however, inconclusive points, since narrative skill may easily account for the first, while the very fact of the transmission of the Narrative through the succeeding centuries would seem to put limits on the influence of 'Davidic idealism'. There is, too, the danger that, in operating with the standard concept of the Succession Narrative, and debating the merits of 'early' and 'late', we may overlook the possibility that the finalized narrative comprises elements of both.

Several features of the narrative have, in fact, been enlisted in support of a post-Solomonic date of origin, though probably only one or two begin to be persuasive, and the most interesting involves emendation of the Hebrew text. In 2 Samuel 13:18 there is an explanatory clause which reads, 'for thus the virgin daughters of the king were dressed in robes', but which Wellhausen emended to read, 'for thus the virgin daughters of the king were dressed in olden days'. The difference in terms of Hebrew consonants is not great—*m'yl(y)m* or *m'wlm*—and, in view of the superior sense which it offers, the emended reading is preferred in several recent English versions. The point to note is that, if the emended reading represents the original form of the text, that original could scarcely be dated to Solomon's reign; a contemporary of Solomon would be unlikely to refer to David's reign as 'olden days'. (A few scholars suggest that the whole clause is interpolative, but this would be difficult to prove.)

Otto Eissfeldt sought to justify a post-Solomonic dating partly on the basis of an alternative Septuagint version of 2 Samuel 20:18f., which can be retroverted into Hebrew and then translated, 'Ask in Abel and in Dan whether anything that the faithful of Israel have laid down has failed'. This, according to Eissfeldt, recognizes that these two Israelite cities remained loyal to Israelite traditions even when they came under Aramaean domination in the ninth century. However, the Septuagint reading is not so obviously superior as is sometimes suggested. It is also unlikely that, after the secession of the northern tribes, Dan of all places would be acknowledged by a Judaean writer as a repository of pure Israelite tradition (cf. 1 Kgs 12:28ff.)!

It would also be possible to press 2 Samuel 18:18 to the disadvantage of a Solomonic dating of the Succession Narrative, inasmuch as the words 'to this day' naturally imply the elapse of a considerable period of time between act and comment on the act. 2 Samuel 20:2, it would seem, also contains a likely pointer to a post-Solomonic dating. The background to the verse is the dispute between Israel and Judah as to whose should have been the honour of conducting David back over the Jordan, after the collapse of Absalom's rebellion. The men of Israel thought that they should have had the privilege, since they had been 'the first to speak of bringing back *our* king' (19:43). Pre-empted by the men of Judah, and not a little annoyed in consequence, they are depicted in 20:2 as readily falling in with Sheba's call to defect: 'So all the men of Israel withdrew from David and followed Sheba the son of Bichri; but the men of Judah followed *their* king steadfastly from the Jordan to Jerusalem'. In the circumstances it is not difficult to see this as a fairly heavy editorial intervention in the dispute between the two parties, and the question to be answered is whether a writer in Solomon's reign would have expressed himself thus, when the split between the north and south had not yet been institutionalized. Certainly, a writer composing his account after the secession of the northerners might well suggest adumbrations of the later event in the unsuccessful rebellion led by Sheba. (It scarcely requires mentioning that the slogan attributed to Sheba in 2 Sam. 20:1 is repeated in a slightly different form in 1 Kgs 12:16, there with a significant augment giving it a dynastic dimension.) A further point of contact between 2 Samuel 19-20 and 1 Kings 12 is the use of the root *qāšāh* ('to be difficult, harsh') in connection with the altercation between the men of Judah and the men of Israel in the one case, and the harsh response of Rehoboam to the protests of the men of Israel in the other ('were fiercer' [2 Sam. 19:43]; 'harshly' [1 Kgs 12:13]).

Further Reading

Pride of place must go to Rost's study:

> Rost, 65-114.

For a discussion of the Succession Narrative as a historical composition from the period of the so-called 'Solomonic Enlightenment' see:

> G. von Rad, 'The Beginnings of Historical Writing in Ancient Israel', in *The Problem of the Hexateuch and Other Essays* (ET), Edinburgh/London: Oliver and Boyd, 1966, 166-204.

A volume which deals extensively with the chapters comprised in the Succession Narrative is:

> R.A. Carlson, *David, the Chosen King. A Traditio-Historical Approach to the Second Book of Samuel*, Stockholm: Almqvist and Wiksell, 1964.

Questions of purpose and theme are treated in:

> J. Blenkinsopp, 'Theme and Motif in the Succession History (2 Sam. XI 2ff) and the Yahwist Corpus', *VTS* 15 (1966), 44-57.

> W. Brueggemann, 'David and his Theologian', *CBQ* 30 (1968), 156-181.

Brueggemann, 'On Trust and Freedom. A Study of Faith in the Succession Narrative', *Interpretation* 26 (1972), 3-19.

Brueggemann, *In Man We Trust*, Atlanta: John Knox Press, 1972, 29-47.

J.W. Flanagan, 'Court History or Succession Document? A Study of 2 Samuel 9-20 and 1 Kings 1-2', *JBL* 91 (1972), 172-181.

H. Hagan, 'Deception as Motif and Theme in 2 Sm 9-20; 1 Kgs 1-2', *Biblica* 60 (1979), 301-326.

J.A. Wharton, 'A Plausible Tale: Story and Theology in II Samuel 9-20, I Kings 1-2', *Interpretation* 35 (1981), 341-354.

P.K. McCarter, Jr, ' "Plots, True and False": The Succession Narrative as Court Apologetic', *Interpretation* 35 (1981), 355-367.

For discussion of the wisdom affinities of the Succession Narrative see:

R.N. Whybray, *The Succession Narrative. A Study of II Sam. 9-20 and I Kings 1 and 2* (SBT, II/9), London: SCM Press, 1968.

Whybray, *The Intellectual Tradition in the Old Testament* (BZAW, 135), Berlin/New York: Walter de Gruyter, 1974, 89-91.

J.L. Crenshaw, 'Method in Determining Wisdom Influence upon "Historical" Literature', *JBL* 88 (1969), 129-142.

H.-J. Hermisson, 'Weisheit und Geschichte', in *Probleme biblischer Theologie* (Fs G. von Rad; ed. H.W. Wolff), München: Kaiser, 1971, 136-154.

J.A. Soggin, in Hayes—Miller, 337f.

Crüsemann, 180-193.

Studies of literary and structural aspects of the Succession Narrative include:

D.M. Gunn, 'Traditional Composition in the "Succession Narrative"', *VT* 26 (1976), 214-229.

Gunn, *The Story of King David. Genre and Interpretation* (*JSOT* Suppl., 6), Sheffield: JSOT Press, 1978.

J. van Seters, 'Problems in the Literary Analysis of the Court History of David', *JSOT* 1 (1976), 22-29.

C. Conroy, *Absalom Absalom! Narrative and Language in 2 Sam 13-20* (Analecta Biblica, 81), Rome: Biblical Institute Press, 1978.

J.P. Fokkelman, *Narrative Art and Poetry in the Books of Samuel, I: King David (II Sam. 9-20 & I Kings 1-2)*, Assen: van Gorcum, 1981.

G.W. Coats, 'Parable, Fable, and Anecdote. Storytelling in the Succession Narrative', *Interpretation* 35 (1981), 368-382.

The exponents of *Tendenz*-criticism write mainly in German:

L. Delekat, 'Tendenz und Theologie der David-Salomo-Erzählung', in *Das ferne und nahe Wort* (Fs L. Rost; BZAW, 105; ed. F. Maass), Berlin: Alfred Töpelmann, 1967, 26-36.

E. Würthwein, *Die Erzählung von der Thronfolge Davids— theologische oder politische Geschichtsschreibung?* (Theologische Studien, 115), Zürich: Theologischer Verlag, 1974.

T. Veijola, *Die ewige Dynastie. David und die Entstehung seiner Dynastie nach der deuteronomistischen Darstellung*, Helsinki: Suomalainen Tiedeakatemia, 1975.

Or in French:

F. Langlamet, 'Pour ou Contre Salomon? La Rédaction Pro-salomonienne de I Rois, I-II', *RB* 83 (1976), 321-379, 481-528.

For historical aspects of the reign of David see:

J. Bright, *A History of Israel* (3rd edn), Philadelphia: Westminster / London: SCM Press, 1981, 195-211.

J.A. Soggin, in Hayes—Miller, 350-363.

For a fairly recent defence of the Succession Narrative as propounded by Rost see:

T. Ishida, 'Solomon's Succession to the Throne of David—A Political Analysis', in *Studies in the Period of David and Solomon and Other Essays* (ed. T. Ishida), Tokyo: Yamakawa-Shuppansha, 1982, 175-187.

Discussion of the Succession Narrative as 'history' within the wider context of Old Testament history-writing may be found in:

J. van Seters, 'Histories and Historians of the Ancient Near East: The Israelites', *Orientalia* NS 50 (1981), 156-167.

For a recent discussion of the problems involved in maintaining the Succession Narrative as a separate literary entity see:

> P.R. Ackroyd, 'The Succession Narrative (so-called)', *Interpretation* 35 (1981), 383-396.

Other studies mentioned in the above discussion:

> O. Eissfeldt, *The Old Testament: An Introduction* (ET), New York: Harper & Row / Oxford: Blackwell, 1965, 137-141.

> M. Noth, *Könige 1* (BKAT, 9/1), Neukirchen-Vluyn: Neukirchener Verlag, 1968, 9-13.

> Gray, 14-22.

> Mettinger, 27-32.

9

THE SAMUEL
APPENDIX
(2 SAMUEL 21-24)

COMPARED with the neatly ligatured narratives of the preceding chapters, 2 Samuel 21-24 is more in the nature of a miscellany of pieces relating to different periods within David's reign. The compiler's disinclination to integrate these episodes, poems, and lists into the main narrative could be used as an argument for the prior existence of the so-called 'Succession Narrative', which was considered altogether too compact to admit of insertions. But, as we saw in the previous chapter, that is a complex issue. On the other hand, it is easy to see why the compiler decided to position these traditions relating to David after ch. 20, since what follows in 1 Kings 1-2 is really an interleaving of the biographies of David and Solomon. It also enables the appendix to be seen as a fitting summary of David's reign, for when the story resumes in 1 Kings 1 David is a pathetic shadow of his former self.

Variegated the material may be, but at least since the publication of Budde's commentary it has been recognized that the manner in which it is arranged is anything but haphazard, as will be apparent from the following list of headings: (1) famine story (21:1-14); (2) warrior exploits (21:15-22); (3) psalm (22:2-51); (4) oracle (23:1-7); (5) warrior exploits and warrior list (23:8-39); (6) plague story (24:1-25). It looks as if the concentric structure, with pairing of items 1 and 6, 2 and 5, and 3 and 4, is the deliberate creation of the compiler. Not that it could be missed in any case, but the thematic parallel between the famine and the plague stories is actually drawn to our attention by the use of the word 'again' in 24:1, and by the matching statements, in 21:14 and 24:25, that God 'heeded supplications for the land'.

As Hertzberg has noted, it made good sense from the compiler's point of view to place the Gibeonite episode at the beginning, since it has a bearing on an important question in previous chapters, viz. David's relations with the depleted house of Saul, and presumably relates to the earlier part of David's reign. It is often urged, indeed, that 21:1-14 is chronologically anterior to ch. 9, and that the surrender of the seven 'sons' of Saul to the Gibeonites was what inspired Shimei's denunciation of David as a 'man of blood' (2 Sam. 16:7). Common-sense considerations would also dictate that the plague story, which literally prepares the ground for the building of Solomon's temple—at least, if we follow the Chronicler—, should be stationed as near as possible to the account of Solomon's reign at the beginning of 1 Kings. In the case of the Gibeonite episode in 21:1-14 there are also obvious phraseological and thematic links with ch. 20 which do not appear to be attributable in their entirety to editorial twinning of the narratives, and which may, therefore, have something to say about the composition of 2 Samuel. Carlson was sufficiently impressed by the links between 21:1-14 and chs 9-20 as a whole to argue that 21:1-14 really belongs to the (so-called) 'Succession Narrative', albeit his explanation of the present position of the narrative is based on an idiosyncratic under-standing of the significance of 2 Samuel 12:6, in its Septuagintal form, for the composition of 2 Samuel.

Forming the centre-piece of the 'appendix' are the poems of 22:2-51 and 23:1-7, the former reviewing the mighty acts of God for, and through, David, and the latter expressing the assurance of an enduring Davidic dynasty. The long psalm which occupies ch. 22 quickly progresses from recollection of a day of distress (vv. 5-7) to a celebration of the divine power and goodness that have given David victory over all his enemies. In this picture of success at every turn the glory is unreservedly ascribed to God, and, as if to insist that this must be so, the register of heroic exploits which precedes the psalm recalls an occasion when, wearied by his exertions in the battle, David almost fell foul of a Philistine warrior. To his men he might be 'the lamp of Israel' and irreplaceable (21:17), but his psalm declares, 'thou art my lamp, O LORD' (22:29). Divine deliverance supervening upon human weakness is an idea that is also prominent in the summary of warrior exploits which is placed on the other side of the psalmodic centre-piece (23:8-12). It is ironic, therefore, that the concluding scene (24:1ff.) depicts a king proclaiming a census in order to establish the number of his fighting men and the measure of his own importance.

The companion-pieces which stand at the centre of 2 Samuel 21–24 say nothing of the flawed character that was the David who ruled Israel in the early tenth century BC. On the contrary, he is righteous and blameless in the execution of his kingly duties (22:21-25), and can, for the same reason, rejoice in the 'everlasting covenant' which God has made with him and his house (23:3-5). This is the 'Davidic hope', ultimately grounded not in human performance but in divine grace, and it is the seed-bed of Messianism, both Jewish and Christian. But the David who inspired the ideal is not lost to sight, and the fact that the portrait of the ideal is framed with reminders of a human and fallible character shows that the 'David of faith' was not conceived in ignorance of the 'David of history'. What imparts life and meaning to the ideal, in spite of the reality, is the grace that will reinstate the one to whom the promises are made.

Further Reading

K. Budde, *Die Bücher Samuel* (KHAT, VIII), Tübingen/Leipzig: J.C.B. Mohr (Paul Siebeck), 1902, 304.

G.T. Sheppard, *Wisdom as a Hermeneutical Construct. A Study in the Sapientializing of the Old Testament* (BZAW, 151), Berlin/New York: Walter de Gruyter, 1980, 144-158.

Carlson, 194-259.

Hertzberg, 415f.

Veijola, *Dynastie*, 106-126.

Childs, 273-275.

INDEXES

INDEX OF MAIN PASSAGES DISCUSSED

INDEX OF SUBJECTS

INDEX OF AUTHORS